THE
LITTLE
FOXES

ACTING EDITION

— PLAY IN THREE ACTS —

— BY LILLIAN HELLMAN —

**DRAMATISTS
PLAY SERVICE
INC.**

THE LITTLE FOXES
Copyright © Renewed 1967, 1969, Lillian Hellman
Copyright © 1942, Lillian Hellman

Copyright © 1939, Lillian Hellman
Regular Trade Edition

Copyright © 1939, Lillian Hellman
as an unpublished dramatic composition

All Rights Reserved

SPECIAL NOTE

Copy of program of the first performance of *The Little Foxes* as produced at the National Theatre, New York City, February 15, 1939

HERMAN SHUMLIN

presents

TALLULAH BANKHEAD

in

THE LITTLE FOXES

By LILLIAN HELLMAN

WITH PATRICIA COLLINGE AND FRANK CONROY

Staged by Mr. Shumlin
Settings Designed by Howard Bay
Costumes Designed by Aline Bernstein

CAST

(In order of appearance)

	Played by		
ADDIE	"	"	Abbie Mitchell
CAL	"	"	John Marriott
BIRDIE HUBBARD	"	"	Patricia Collinge
OSCAR HUBBARD	"	"	Carl Benton Reid
LEO HUBBARD	"	"	Dan Duryea
REGINA GIDDENS	"	"	Tallulah Bankhead
WILLIAM MARSHALL	"	"	Lee Baker
BENJAMIN HUBBARD	"	"	Charles Dingle
ALEXANDRA GIDDENS	"	"	Florence Williams
HORACE GIDDENS	"	"	Frank Conroy

SYNOPSIS OF SCENES

The scene of the play is the living-room of the Giddens House, a small town in the South.

ACT I: The spring of 1900, evening.

ACT II: A week later, early morning.

ACT III: Two weeks later, late afternoon.

There has been no attempt to write Southern dialect. It is to be understood that the accents are Southern.

3

THE LITTLE FOXES

ACT I

SCENE: *The living-room of the Giddens house, a small town in the deep South, the spring of 1900. Upstage is a staircase leading to the second story.* U. R. *are double doors to the dining-room. When these doors are open we see a section of the dining room and the furniture.* U. L. *is an entrance hall with a coat-rack and umbrella stand. There are large lace-curtained windows on the* L. *wall. The room is lit by a center gas chandelier and painted china oil lamps on the tables. Against the wall is a large piano.* D. R. *is a high couch, a large table, several chairs. Against the* L. *back wall is a table and several chairs. Near the window there is a smaller couch and tables. The room is good-looking, the furniture expensive, but it reflects no particular taste. Everything is of the best, and that is all.*

AT RISE: ADDIE, *a tall, nice-looking Negro woman of about fifty-five, is closing the* U. S. *windows. From behind the closed dining-room doors there is the sound of voices. After a second* CAL, *a middle-aged Negro, comes in from the entrance* L. *hall, carrying a tray with 10 glasses and a bottle of port wine.* ADDIE *crosses, takes the tray from him, puts it on table, begins to arrange it.*

ADDIE. (*Pointing to bottle.*) You gone stark out of your head?
CAL. No, smart lady, I ain't. Miss Regina told me to get out that bottle (*points to bottle*), that very bottle for the mighty honored guest. When Miss Regina changes orders like that you can bet your dime she got her reason.
ADDIE. (*Points to dining-room—not looking.*) Go on. You'll be needed. (*She arranges glasses and pours wine.*)

5

CAL. (*Looking at* ADDIE *while wiping glasses.*) Miss Zan she had two helpings frozen fruit cream and she tell that honored guest, she tell him that you make the (*steps down to* ADDIE) best frozen fruit cream in all the South.

ADDIE. (*Smiles, pleased.*) Did she? Well, see that Belle saves a little for her. She like it right before she go to bed. Save a few little cakes, too, she like —— (*Dining-room doors are opened and quickly closed again by* BIRDIE HUBBARD. BIRDIE *is a woman of about forty, with a pretty, well-bred, faded face. Her movements are usually nervous and timid, but now, as she comes running into the room, she is gay and excited.* CAL *turns to* BIRDIE.)

BIRDIE. Oh, Cal. (*Closes door.*) I want you to get one of the kitchen boys to run home for me. He's to look in my desk drawer and —— (*Crosses* D. *to back of chair* R. C. *to* ADDIE.) My, Addie. What a good supper. Just as good as good can be.

ADDIE. You look pretty this evening, Miss Birdie, and young.

BIRDIE. (*Laughing.*) Me, young? (*Turns back to* CAL.) Maybe you better find Simon and tell him to do it himself. He's to look in my desk, the left drawer, and bring my music album right away. Mr. Marshall is very anxious to see it because of his father and the opera in Chicago. (*To* ADDIE.) Mr. Marshall is such a polite man with his manners, and very educated and cultured, and I've told him all about how my Mama and Papa used to go to Europe for the music —— (*Laughs. To* ADDIE.) Imagine going all the way to Europe just to listen to music. Wouldn't that be nice, Addie? Just to sit there and listen and —— (*Turns and takes step to* CAL.) Left drawer, Cal. Tell him that twice because he forgets. And tell him not to let any of the things drop out of the album and to bring it right in here when he comes back. (*Dining-room doors are opened and quickly closed by* OSCAR HUBBARD. *He is a man in his late forties.*)

CAL. Yes'm. But Simon he won't get it right. (*Crossing to door* L.) But I'll tell him.

BIRDIE. Left drawer, Cal, and tell him to bring the blue book and ——

OSCAR. (*Sharply.*) Birdie.

BIRDIE. (*Turning nervously.*) Oh, Oscar, I was just sending Simon for my music album.

OSCAR. (*To* CAL, *who has stopped at door* L. *to listen.*) Never mind about the album. Miss Birdie has changed her mind.

6

BIRDIE. But, really, Oscar. Really I promised Mr. Marshall. I ——
(CAL *looks at them, exits* L.)

OSCAR. Why do you leave the dinner table and go running about like a child? (ADDIE *crosses around sofa to* D. S. *window, closes windows.*)

BIRDIE. (*Trying to be gay.*) But, Oscar, Mr. Marshall said most specially he *wanted* to see my album. I told him about the time Mama met Wagner and Mrs. Wagner gave her the signed program and the big picture. (OSCAR *moves away* D. C.) Mr. Marshall wants to see that. (BIRDIE *moves to him.*) Very, very much. We had such a nice talk and ——

OSCAR. (*Taking step to her.*) You have been chattering to him like a magpie. You haven't let him be for a second. I can't think he came South to be bored with you. (*He turns away, crosses* D. R.)

BIRDIE. (*Quickly, hurt.*) He wasn't bored. I don't believe he was bored. He's a very educated, cultured gentleman. (*Her voice rises.*) I just don't believe it. (ADDIE *moves up to back of sofa.*) You always talk like that when I'm having a nice time.

OSCAR. (*Turning to her, sharply.*) You have had too much wine. Get yourself in hand now.

BIRDIE. (*Drawing back, about to cry, shrilly.*) What am I doing? I am not doing anything. (ADDIE *crosses* U. *back of sofa.*) What am I doing?

OSCAR. (*Taking a step to her, tensely.*) I said get yourself in hand. Stop acting like a fool. (ADDIE *crosses to* U. S. *windows, closes them.*)

BIRDIE. (*Moves up, then turns to him, quietly.*) I don't believe he was bored. I just don't believe it. Some people like music and like to talk about it. (LEO *enters from dining-room.* REGINA *in dining-room rings bell.*) That's all I was doing. (LEO HUBBARD *comes hurrying through the door. He is a young man of twenty, with a weak kind of good looks.*)

LEO. Mama! (BIRDIE *turns sharply to him.*) Papa. They are coming in now.

OSCAR. (*Softly, stepping up to* BIRDIE.) Sit down, Birdie. Sit down now. (OSCAR *crosses* D. R. LEO *crosses* D. L. *to piano.* BIRDIE *sits down in chair* L. C., *bows her head as if to hide her face. Dining room doors are opened by* CAL. *We see people beginning to rise from the table.* REGINA GIDDENS *comes in with* WILLIAM MARSHALL. REGINA *is a handsome woman of forty.* MARSHALL *is forty-five,*

7

pleasant looking, self-possessed. Behind them comes ALEXANDRA
GIDDENS, *a very pretty, rather delicate looking girl of seventeen.
She is followed by* BENJAMIN HUBBARD, *fifty-five, with a large
jovial face and the light graceful movements that one often finds
in large men.* REGINA, *after a sharp look at* BIRDIE *and* OSCAR,
crosses to sofa R. MARSHALL *crosses* C. *to chair* R. C. ALEXANDRA
crosses D. L. *to settee and sits.*)

REGINA. Mr. Marshall, I think you're trying to console me. Chicago
may be the noisiest, dirtiest city in the world but I should still
prefer it to the sound of our horses and the smell of our azaleas.
I should like crowds of people, and theaters, and lovely
women —— (REGINA *sits on sofa, smiles at* MARSHALL *and indicates for him to sit next to her.*) *V*ery lovely women, Mr. Marshall? (BEN *crosses to back of settee* L.)

MARSHALL. (*Crossing to sofa* R.) In Chicago? Oh, I suppose so.
But I can tell you this: I've never dined there with three *such*
lovely ladies. (*He sits on sofa to* R. *of* REGINA. ADDIE *comes down
to table, takes bottle off tray and serves wine.*)

BEN. (*Crossing to* C., *nods.*) Our Southern women are well fa-
vored.

LEO. (*Stepping in, laughs.*) But one must go to Mobile for the
ladies, sir. Very elegant worldly ladies, too. (ADDIE *is serving*
REGINA, *who hands a glass to* MARSHALL, *then takes one for herself.*)

BEN. (*Looks at him very deliberately.*) Worldly, eh? Worldly,
did you say? (ADDIE *serves* BEN.)

OSCAR. (*Hastily, to* LEO.) Your Uncle Ben means that worldliness
is not a mark of beauty in any woman.

LEO. (*Steps up to above settee* L. *Quickly.*) Of course, Uncle Ben.
I didn't mean —— (BEN *crosses* R. *to chair* R. C., *sits.*)

MARSHALL. Your port is excellent, Mrs. Giddens. (ADDIE *serves*
BIRDIE, *who catches* OSCAR's *look at her, and refuses the drink.*)

REGINA. Thank you, Mr. Marshall. We had been saving that bottle, hoping we could open it just for you.

ALEXANDRA. (*As* ADDIE *comes to her with tray.*) Oh. May I *really*,
Addie?

ADDIE. Better ask Mama.

ALEXANDRA. May I, Mama?

REGINA. (*Nods, smiles.*) In Mr. Marshall's honor.

ALEXANDRA. (Smiles.) Mr. Marshall, this will be the first taste of port I've ever had. (ADDIE serves LEO.)

MARSHALL. (Leaning forward.) No one ever had their first taste of a better port. (He lifts his glass in a toast, she lifts hers, they both drink. Sits back. Looks around the room, smiles. ADDIE crosses to OSCAR U. R., serves him.) Well, I suppose it is all true, Mrs. Giddens. (OSCAR crosses D. R.)

REGINA. What is true? (ADDIE crosses to table for bottle, takes the tray to table U. C., places it there, then exits L.)

MARSHALL. That you Southerners occupy a unique position in America. You live better than the rest of us, you eat better, you drink better. I wonder you find time, or want to find time, to do business.

BEN. (Laughs.) A great many Southerners don't.

MARSHALL. Do all of you live here together?

REGINA. Here with me? (Laughs.) Oh, no. My brother Ben lives next door. My brother Oscar and his family live in the next square.

BEN. (Sitting forward.) But we are a very close family. We've always wanted it that way.

MARSHALL. That is very pleasant. Keeping your family together to share each other's lives. My family moves around too much. My children seem never to come home. Away at school in the winter; in the summer, Europe with their mother —— (BEN sits back.)

REGINA. (Eagerly.) Oh, yes. Even down here we read about Mrs. Marshall in the society pages.

MARSHALL. I dare say. She moves about a great deal. And all of you are part of the same business? Hubbard Sons?

BEN. (Motions to OSCAR.) Oscar and me. (Motions to REGINA.) My sister's good husband is a banker.

MARSHALL. (Looks at REGINA, surprised.) Oh.

REGINA. I am so sorry that my husband isn't here to meet you. He's been very ill. He is at Johns Hopkins. But he will be home soon. We think he is getting better now.

LEO. (Crosses to above chair L. C.) I work for Uncle Horace. (REGINA looks at him.) I mean I work for Uncle Horace at his bank. I keep an eye on things while he's away.

REGINA. (Smiles.) Really, Leo?

9

BEN. (*Looks at him, then to* MARSHALL.) Modesty in the young is as excellent as it is rare. (*Looks at* LEO *again.*)

OSCAR. (*To* LEO.) Your Uncle means that a young man should speak more modestly.

LEO. (*Hastily, taking a step to* BEN.) Oh, I didn't mean, sir ——

MARSHALL. Oh, Mrs. Hubbard. Where's that Wagner autograph you promised to let me see? My train will be leaving soon and —— (LEO *crosses* U. *to table* U. C., *pours himself a drink.*)

BIRDIE. The autograph? Oh. Well. Really, Mr. Marshall, I didn't mean to chatter so about it. Really I —— (*Nervously, looking at* OSCAR.) You must excuse me. I didn't get it because, well, because I had—I—I had a little headache and ——

OSCAR. My wife is a miserable victim of headaches. (*Crosses* U. R. *to above sofa* R.)

REGINA. (*Quickly.*) Mr. Marshall said at supper that he would like you to play for him, Alexandra.

ALEXANDRA. (*Who has been looking at* BIRDIE.) It's not I who play well, sir. It's my aunt. She plays just wonderfully. She's my teacher. (*Rises, eagerly.*) May we play a duet? May we, Mama?

BIRDIE. (*Taking* ALEXANDRA'S *hand.*) Thank you, dear. But I have my headache now. I ——

OSCAR. (*Sharply.*) Don't be stubborn, Birdie. Mr. Marshall wants you to play.

MARSHALL. Indeed I do. If your headache isn't ——

BIRDIE. (*Hesitates, then gets up, pleased.*) But I'd like to, sir. Very much. (*She and* ALEXANDRA *go to piano.* ALEXANDRA *brings chair from* U. L. *corner to piano for herself.* BIRDIE *moves stool* D. S., *then takes some music from top of piano. They talk about the music for a second, then study it.* OSCAR *slowly crosses* L. *to chair* L. C.)

MARSHALL. It's very remarkable how you Southern aristocrats have kept together. Kept together and kept what belonged to you.

BEN. You misunderstand, sir. Southern aristocrats have *not* kept together and have *not* kept what belonged to them.

MARSHALL. (*Laughs, indicates room.*) You don't call this keeping what belongs to you? (OSCAR *sits chair* L. C.)

BEN. But we are not aristocrats. (LEO *slowly crosses* R. *to* D. R.— *listening. Points to* BIRDIE *at piano.*) Our brother's wife is the only one of us who belongs to the Southern aristocracy. (BIRDIE *selects a book of music. She opens it as* ALEXANDRA *sits down. She is*

stopped by " our brother's wife," looks toward BEN. ALEXANDRA
looks up at her.)

MARSHALL. (*Smiles.*) My information is that you people have been
here, and solidly here, for a long time. (BIRDIE *turns back and goes
through the pages.*)

OSCAR. And so we have. Since our great-grandfather.

BEN. (*Smiles.*) Who was *not* an aristocrat, like Birdie's.

MARSHALL. (*A little sharply.*) You make great distinctions. (BIRDIE
*has found page, and looks up again on " like Birdie's." ALEXANDRA
turns head a little to them. BIRDIE turns back to music. LEO is D. R.*)

BEN. Oh, they have been made for us. And maybe they are important distinctions. (*Leans forward, intimately.*) Now you take
Birdie's family. When my great-grandfather came here they were
the highest tone plantation owners in this state. (BIRDIE *looks at
them. ALEXANDRA looks back to her, takes her hand, pats it.*)

LEO. (*Steps to MARSHALL. Proudly.*) My mother's grandfather
was governor of the state before the war. (BIRDIE *turns back to*
ALEXANDRA.)

OSCAR. They owned the plantation, Lionnet. You may have heard
of it, sir?

MARSHALL. (*Laughs.*) No, I've never heard of anything but brick
houses on a lake, and *cotton mills.*

BEN. Lionnet in its day was the best cotton land in the South. It
still brings us in a fair crop. (*Sits back.*) Ah, they were great days
for those people—even when I can remember. They had the best
of everything. (BIRDIE *turns to them.*) Cloth from Paris, trips to
Europe, horses you can't raise any more, niggers to lift their
fingers ——

BIRDIE. (*Suddenly.*) We were good to our people. Everybody knew
that. We were better to them than —— (MARSHALL *looks up at*
BIRDIE.)

REGINA. (*A quick look at MARSHALL, then to BIRDIE.*) Why,
Birdie. You aren't playing. (MARSHALL *has been looking curiously
at* BIRDIE.)

BEN. But when the war comes these fine gentlemen ride off and
leave the cotton, *and* the women, to rot.

BIRDIE. My father was killed in the war. He was a fine soldier, Mr.
Marshall. A fine man.

REGINA. Oh, certainly, Birdie. A famous soldier.

BEN. (*To BIRDIE.*) But that isn't the tale I am telling Mr. Marshall.

(*To* MARSHALL.) Well, sir, the war ends. (BIRDIE *goes back to piano, puts down music, sits and is ready to play.*) Lionnet is almost ruined, and the sons finish ruining it. And there were thousands like them. Why? (*Leans forward.*) Because the Southern aristocrat can adapt himself to nothing. Too high-toned to try.

MARSHALL. Sometimes it is difficult to learn new ways. (BIRDIE *and* ALEXANDRA *begin to play.* MARSHALL *leans forward, listening.*)

BEN. Perhaps, perhaps. (*All listen to music. He sees that* MARSHALL *is paying attention to the music. Irritated, he turns to* BIRDIE *and* ALEXANDRA *at piano, then back to* MARSHALL.) You're right, Mr. Marshall. It is difficult to learn new ways. But maybe that's why it's profitable. Our grandfather and our father learn the new ways and learned how to make them pay. They work. (*Smiles nastily.*) They are in trade. Hubbard Sons, Merchandise. Others, Birdie's family for example, look down on them. (*Settles back in chair.*) To make a long story short, Lionnet now belongs to us. (BIRDIE *stops playing and turns to them.*) Twenty years ago we took over their land, their cotton, and their daughter. (BIRDIE *rises and stands stiffly by piano.* MARSHALL, *who has been watching her, rises.*)

MARSHALL. May I bring you a glass of port, Mrs. Hubbard?

BIRDIE. (*Softly.*) No, thank you, sir. You are most polite. (*She turns away and sits.* ALEXANDRA *tries to soothe her and asks her to play again. She pantomimes that she cannot, and for* ALEXANDRA *to play alone.*)

REGINA. (*Sharply, to* BEN.) You are boring Mr. Marshall with these ancient family tales.

BEN. I hope not. I hope not. I am trying to make an important point—(*Bows to* MARSHALL.) for our future business partner. (MARSHALL *sits.*)

OSCAR. (*To* MARSHALL.) My brother always says that it's folks like us who have struggled and fought to bring to our land some of the prosperity of your land.

BEN. Some people call that patriotism.

REGINA. (*Laughs gaily.*) I hope you don't find my brothers too obvious, Mr. Marshall. I'm afraid they mean that this is the time for the ladies to leave the gentlemen to talk business.

MARSHALL. (*Hastily.*) Not at all. We settled everything this afternoon. (ALEXANDRA *starts to play, alone.* MARSHALL *looks at hi-*

watch.) I have only a few minutes before I must leave for the train. *Smiles at her.*) And I insist they be spent with you.

REGINA. *And* with another glass of port.

MARSHALL. Thank you. (REGINA *looks at him, smiles, gets up, takes his glass and crosses to table* U. C. MARSHALL *rises when she does, then sits.*)

BEN. (*To* REGINA *as she passes him.*) My sister is right. (*To* MARSHALL.) I am a plain man and I am trying to say a plain thing. (*Sitting forward.*) A man ain't only in business for what he can get out of it. It's got to give him something here. (*Puts hand to his breast.* REGINA *pours* MARSHALL'S *drink.*) That's every bit as true for the nigger picking cotton for a silver quarter, as it is for you and me. (REGINA *hands* MARSHALL *glass, then sits.*) If it don't give him something here, then he don't pick the cotton right. (*Sits back.* REGINA *crosses* D. *to sofa.*) Money isn't all. Not by three shots.

MARSHALL. Really? Well, I always thought it was a great deal. (*Drinks.*)

REGINA. And so did I, Mr. Marshall.

MARSHALL. (*Leans forward. Pleasantly, but with meaning.*) Now you don't have to convince me that you are the right people for the deal. I wouldn't be here if you hadn't convinced me six months ago. You want the mill here, and I want it here. It isn't my business to find out *why* you want it.

BEN. To bring the machine to the cotton, and not the cotton to the machine.

MARSHALL. (*Amused.*) You have a turn for neat phrases, Hubbard. Well, however grand your reasons are, mine are simple: (LEO *crosses* U. C. *to table—pours drink.*) I want to make money and I believe I'll make it on you. (*As* BEN *starts to speak, he smiles.*) Mind you, I have no objections to more high minded reasons. They are mighty valuable in business. It's fine to have partners who so closely follow the teachings of Christ. (*Gets up.*) And now I must leave for my train. (*Puts his glass on table. All except* BIRDIE *rise.* ALEXANDRA *stops playing.*)

REGINA. I'm sorry you won't stay over with us, Mr. Marshall, but you'll come again, any time you like.

BEN. (*Motions to* LEO, *indicating bottle.*) Fill them up, boy, fill them up. (LEO *moves around, filling glasses as* BEN *speaks.*) Down here, sir, we have a strange custom. We drink the *last* drink for a toast. That's to prove that the Southerner is always still on his feet for the last drink. (*Picks up his glass.*) It was Henry Frick, your Mr. Henry Frick, who said, "Railroads are the Rembrandts of investments." Well, I say, "Southern cotton mills *will be the* Rembrandts of investments." So I give you the firm of Hubbard Sons and Marshall, Cotton Mills, and to it a long and prosperous life. (*They all pick up their glasses.* MARSHALL *looks at them, amused. Then he, too, lifts his glass, smiles.*)

OSCAR. The children will drive you to the depot. (*Crosses to table* U. C.—*puts down glass.*) Leo! Alexandra! You will drive Mr. Marshall down.

LEO. (*Eagerly, looks at* BEN *who nods.*) Yes, sir. (*To* MARSHALL.) Not often Uncle Ben lets me drive the horses. And a beautiful pair they are. (*Starts for hall.*) Come on, Zan. (*Exits.*)

ALEXANDRA. (*Crosses to* BEN.) May I drive tonight, Uncle Ben, please? I'd like to and ——

BEN. (*Shakes his head, laughs.*) In your evening clothes? Oh, no, my dear.

ALEXANDRA. But Leo always —— (*Stops, exits quickly.*)

REGINA. I don't like to say good-bye to you, Mr. Marshall.

MARSHALL. Then we won't say good-bye. You have promised that you would come and let me show you Chicago. Do I have to make you promise again?

REGINA. (*Looks at him as he presses her hand.*) I promise again. (BEN *crosses to hall.*)

MARSHALL. (*Touches her hand again, then moves to* BIRDIE.) Good-bye, Mrs. Hubbard. (BIRDIE *rises, crosses* C.)

BIRDIE. (*Shyly, with sweetness and dignity.*) Good-bye, sir. (*He bows, starts toward entrance hall.* REGINA *crosses to* C.)

MARSHALL. (*As he passes* REGINA.) Remember.

REGINA. I will.

OSCAR. We'll see you to the carriage. (MARSHALL *exits followed by* OSCAR. *For a second* REGINA *and* BIRDIE *stand looking after them. Then* REGINA *throws up her arms, laughs happily.*)

REGINA. And there, Birdie, goes the man who has opened the door to our future.

BIRDIE. (*Surprised at the unaccustomed friendliness.*) What?

REGINA. (*Turning to her.*) Our future. Yours and mine, Ben's and Oscar's, the children's —— (*Looks at* BIRDIE's *puzzled face, laughs.*) Our future! (*After a second crosses* D. L. *to* BIRDIE.)

14

You were charming at supper, Birdie. Mr. Marshall certainly thought so.

BIRDIE. (*Pleased.*) Why, Regina. Do you think he did?

REGINA. Can't you tell when you're being admired?

BIRDIE. Oscar said I bored Mr. Marshall. (*Then quickly.*) But he admired *you*. He told me so.

REGINA. What did he say?

BIRDIE. He said to me, "I hope your sister-in-law will come to Chicago. Chicago will be at her feet." He said the ladies would bow to your manners and the gentlemen to your looks.

REGINA. (*Crossing* R. *to sofa.*) Did he? He seems a lonely man. Imagine being lonely with all that money. I don't think he likes his wife.

BIRDIE. Not like his wife? What a thing to say.

REGINA. (*Sits sofa* R.) She's away a great deal. He said that several times. And once he made fun of her being so social and high-toned. But that fits in all right. (*Sits back, arms on back of sofa, stretches.*) Her being social, I mean. She can introduce me. It won't take long with an introduction from her.

BIRDIE. (*Bewildered.*) Introduce you? In Chicago? You mean you really might go? (*Crosses* R. *to table.*) Oh, Regina, you can't leave here. What about Horace?

REGINA. Don't look so scared about everything, Birdie. I'm going to live in Chicago. I've always wanted to. And now there'll be plenty of money to go with.

BIRDIE. (*Sits chair* R. C.) But Horace won't be able to move around. You know what the doctor wrote.

REGINA. There'll be millions, Birdie, millions. You know what I've always said when people told me we were rich? I said I think you should either be a nigger or a millionaire. In between, like us, what for? (*Laughs. Look at* BIRDIE.) But I'm not going away tomorrow, Birdie. (*Takes her arms down.*) There's plenty of time to worry about Horace when he comes home. If he ever decides to come home.

BIRDIE. Will we be going to Chicago? I mean, Oscar and Leo and me?

REGINA. You? I shouldn't think so. (*Laughs. Leaning forward.*) Well, we must remember tonight. It's a very important night and we mustn't forget it. We shall plan all the things we'd like to have and then we'll really have them. Make a wish, Birdie, any wish. It's bound to come true now. (BEN *and* OSCAR *enter.*)

BIRDIE. (*Laughs.*) Well. Well, I don't know. Maybe. (REGINA *turns to look at* BEN.) Well, I guess I'd know right off what I wanted. (BEN *crosses to above* REGINA. OSCAR *stands by upper window, waves to departing carriage.*)

REGINA. (*Looks up at* BEN, *smiles. He smiles back at her.*) Well, you did it. (*Grasps his hand.*)

BEN. Looks like it might be we did.

REGINA. (*Springs up, laughs.*) Looks like it! Don't pretend. (*Rises, crossing* U. C.) You're like a cat who's been licking the cream. (*Crosses to wine bottle on table* U. C.) Now we must all have a drink to celebrate. (BEN *crosses to table* U. C.)

OSCAR. (*From window.*) The children, Alexandra and Leo, make a very handsome couple, Regina. (REGINA *does not look at him.* BEN *and* REGINA *drink.* OSCAR *steps in.*) Marshall remarked himself what fine young folks they were. How well they looked together.

REGINA. (*Sharply.*) Yes. You said that before, Oscar. (*She puts drink down, crosses* D. *to chair* L. C.—*sits.*)

BEN. Yes, sir. (*Crossing* D. R.) It's beginning to look as if the deal's all set. I may not be a subtle man—but —— (*Turns to them. After a second.*) Now somebody ask me how I know the deal is set.

OSCAR. What do you mean, Ben?

BEN. You remember I told him that down here we drink the *last* drink for a toast?

OSCAR. (*Thoughtfully.*) Yes. I never heard that before.

BEN. Nobody's ever heard it before. (*Turns chair* D. R. *to face room. Stands in front of it.*) God forgives those who invent what they need. (*Holding up his glass.*) I already had his signature. But we've all done business with men whose word over a glass is better than a bond. Anyway it don't hurt to have both. (*He sits.*)

OSCAR. (*Turns to* REGINA. *Crosses* L. *to above sofa.*) You understand what Ben means?

REGINA. (*Smiles.*) Yes, Oscar. I understand. I understood immediately.

BEN. (*Looks at her admiringly.*) Did you, Regina? Well, when he lifted his glass to drink, I closed my eyes and saw the bricks going into place.

REGINA. And I saw a lot more than that. (OSCAR *sits sofa* R., *lights cigar, sits back to relax*.)

BEN. Slowly, slowly. As yet we have only our hopes.

REGINA. Birdie and I have just been planning what we want. I know what I want. What will you want, Ben?

BEN. Caution. Don't count the chickens. (*Leans back, laughs.* REGINA *laughs*.) Well, God would allow us a little day dreaming. Good for the soul when you've worked hard enough to deserve it. (*Pauses.*) I think I'll have a stable. For a long time I've had my good eyes on Carter's in Savannah. A rich man's pleasure, the sport of kings, why not the sport of Hubbards? Why not?

REGINA. (*Smiles.*) Why not? What will you have, Oscar?

OSCAR. I don't know. (*Thoughtfully—leaning forward on table.*) The pleasure of seeing the bricks grow will be enough for me.

BEN. Oh, of course. Our *greatest* pleasure will be to see the bricks grow. But we are all entitled to a little side indulgence.

OSCAR. (*Looking front.*) Yes, I suppose so. Well, then, I think we might take a few trips here and there (*to* BIRDIE), eh, Birdie?

BIRDIE. (*Surprised at being consulted.*) Yes, Oscar. I'd like that.

OSCAR. (*Looking front.*) We might even make a regular trip to Jekyll Island. I've heard the Cornelly place is for sale. We might think about buying it. Make a nice change. (*To* BIRDIE.) Do you good, Birdie, a change of climate. (*Front.*) Fine shooting, on Jekyll, the best.

BIRDIE. I'd like ——

OSCAR. (*Indulgently—front.*) What would you like?

BIRDIE. *Two* things. Two things I'd like most.

REGINA. Two! I should like a thousand. You are modest, Birdie.

BIRDIE. (*Warmly, delighted with the unexpected interest.*) I should like to have Lionnet back. I know you own it now, but I'd like to see it fixed up again, the way Mama and Papa had it. Every year it used to get a nice coat of paint—Papa was very particular about the paint—and the lawn was so smooth all the way down to the river, with the trims of zinnias and red-feather plush. And the figs and blue little plums and the scuppernongs —— (*Smiles. Turns to* REGINA.) The organ is still there and it wouldn't cost much to fix. We could have parties for Zan (*Rises, crosses to* REGINA.), the way Mama used to have for me. (*Crosses* U. C., *moving about, dreamily.*)

BEN. That's a pretty picture, Birdie. Might be a most pleasant way to live. (*Dismissing* BIRDIE.) What do you want, Regina?

BIRDIE. (*Very happily, not noticing that they are no longer listening to her, crosses* D. S.) I could have a cutting garden. Just where Mama's used to be. Oh, I do think we could be happier there. Papa used to say that *nobody* had ever lost their temper at Lionnet, and *nobody* ever would. Papa would never let anybody be nasty spoken, or mean. No, sir. (*Moving about* U. C.) He just didn't like it.

BEN. What do you want, Regina?

REGINA. I'm going to Chicago. And when I'm settled there and know the right people and the right things to buy—because I certainly don't now—I shall go to *Paris* and buy them. (*Laughs.*) I'm going to leave you and Oscar to count the bricks.

BIRDIE. (*Turning to* OSCAR, *crosses to chair* R. C.) Oscar. Please let me have Lionnet back.

OSCAR. (*To* REGINA.) You are serious about moving to Chicago? (BIRDIE *crosses* U. *to table* U. C., *pours drink, drinks it fast.*)

BEN. She is going to see the great world and leave us in the little one. Well, we'll come and visit you and meet all the great and be proud to think you are our sister.

REGINA. (*Gaily.*) Certainly. And you won't even have to learn to be subtle, Ben. Stay as you are. You will be rich and the rich don't have to be subtle.

OSCAR. But what about Alexandra? She's seventeen. Old enough to be thinking about marrying.

BIRDIE. (*Crosses* D. *to* OSCAR.) And, Oscar, I have one more wish. Just one more wish.

OSCAR. (*Turns.*) What is it, Birdie? What are you saying?

BIRDIE. I want you to stop shooting. I mean so much. I don't like to see animals and birds killed just for the killing. You only throw them away ——

BEN. (*To* REGINA.) It'll take a great deal of money to live as you're planning, Regina.

REGINA. Certainly. But there'll be plenty of money. You have estimated the profits very high.

BEN. I have ——

BIRDIE. (*Does not notice that* OSCAR *is looking at her furiously.*) And you never let anybody else shoot, and the niggers need it so much to keep from starving. It's wicked to shoot food just because you like to shoot, when poor people need it so ——

BEN. (*Laughs.*) I have estimated the profits very high—for myself.

REGINA. What did you say?

BIRDIE. I've always wanted to speak about it, Oscar.

OSCAR. (*Slowly, carefully.*) What are you chattering about?

BIRDIE. (*Finally catches his tone, nervously.*) I was talking about Lionnet and—and about your shooting ——

OSCAR. You are exciting yourself.

REGINA. (*To* BEN.) I didn't hear you. There was so much talking.

OSCAR. (*To* BIRDIE.) You have been acting very childish, very excited, all evening.

BIRDIE. Regina asked me what I'd like ——

REGINA. What did you say, Ben?

BIRDIE. —now that we'll be so rich. Everybody was saying what they would like, so I said what I would like, too.

BEN. I said —— (*He is interrupted by* OSCAR.)

OSCAR. (*To* BIRDIE.) Very well. We've all heard you. That's enough now.

BEN. I am waiting! (*They stop. Irritated, to* OSCAR.) I am waiting for you to finish. You and Birdie. Four conversations are three too many. (BIRDIE *crosses* U. C. *slowly, sits chair* R. *of table.* OSCAR *nods,* BEN *waits, sees that everything is quiet. Smiles, to* REGINA.) I said that I had, and I do, estimate the profits very high —for myself, and Oscar, of course.

REGINA. (*Slowly.*) And what does that mean? (BEN *shrugs, looks toward* OSCAR.)

OSCAR. (*Looks at* BEN, *clears throat.*) Well, Regina, it's like this. For forty-nine per cent Marshall will put up four hundred thousand dollars. For fifty-one per cent—(*Smiles archly.*) a controlling interest, mind you, we will put up two hundred and twenty-five thousand dollars besides offering him certain benefits that our (*Looks at* BEN *to include him.*) local position allows us to manage. Ben means that two hundred and twenty-five thousand dollars is a lot of money.

REGINA. I know the terms and I know it's a lot of money.

BEN. (*Nodding.*) It is.

OSCAR. Ben means that we are ready with our two-thirds of the money. Your third, Horace's, I mean, doesn't seem to be ready.

(*Raises his hand as* REGINA *starts to speak.*) Ben has written to Horace, I have written, and you have written. He answers. But he **never** mentions this business. Yet we have explained it to him in great detail, and told him the urgency. Still he never mentions it. Ben has been very patient, Regina. (*Sits back.*) Naturally, you are our sister and we want you to benefit from anything we do. (*Looks at* BEN.)

REGINA. (*Rises. To* OSCAR.) And in addition to your concern for me, you do not want control to go out of the family. (*To* BEN.) That right, Ben?

BEN. That's cynical. (*Smiles.*) Cynicism is only an unpleasant way of saying the truth.

OSCAR. (*Rises. Crosses* L. *to* C.) No need to be cynical. We'd have no trouble raising the third share, the share that you want to take.

REGINA. I am sure you could get the third share, the share you were saving for me. But that would give you a strange partner. (*Crosses* R. *to sofa.*) And strange partners sometimes want a great deal. (*Smiles unpleasantly.*) But perhaps it would be wise for you to find him.

OSCAR. (*Turns, step* C.) Now, now. Nobody says we *want* to do that. We would like to have you in and you would like to come in.

REGINA. Yes. I certainly would.

BEN. (*Laughs, puts up his hand.*) But we haven't heard from **Horace.**

REGINA. I've given my word that Horace will put up the money. That should be enough. (OSCAR *crosses to table* D. L., *flicks ash off cigar.*)

BEN. Oh, it was enough. I took your word. But I've got to have more than your word now. The contracts will be signed this week, and Marshall will want to see our money soon after. Regina, Horace has been in Baltimore for five months. I know that you've written him to come home, and that he hasn't come.

OSCAR. It's beginning to look as if he doesn't want to come home.

REGINA. Of course he wants to come home. (*Crossing* C.) You can't move around with heart trouble at any moment you choose. You know what doctors are like once they get their hands on a case like this ——

OSCAR. They can't very well keep him from answering letters, can they? (REGINA *turns to* BEN.) They couldn't keep him from arranging for the money if he wanted to ——

20

REGINA. (*Crossing* R.) Has it occurred to you that Horace is also a good business man?

BEN. Certainly. He is a shrewd trader. Always has been. The bank is proof of that.

REGINA. Then, possibly, he may be keeping silent because he doesn't think he is getting enough for his money. (*Looks at* OSCAR.) Seventy-five thousand he has to put up. That's a lot of money, too. (*Sits sofa.*)

OSCAR. Nonsense. He knows a good thing when he hears it. (*Crosses* R. *to table.*) He knows that we can make *twice* the profit on cotton goods manufactured *here* that can be made in the North.

BEN. That isn't what Regina means. (*Smiles.*) May I interpret you, Regina? (*To* OSCAR.) Regina is saying that Horace wants *more* than a third of our share.

OSCAR. (*Amazed, playing along.*) But he's only putting up a third of the money. You put up a third and you get a third. What else could he expect?

REGINA. Well, I don't know. I don't know about these things. It would seem that if you put up a third you should only get a third. But then again, there's no law about it, is there? (OSCAR *turns—crosses to chair* L. C.) I should think that if you knew your money was very badly needed, well, you just might say, I want more, I want a bigger share. (OSCAR *turns—crosses* U. *back of sofa* L.) You *boys* have done that. I've heard you say so.

BEN. (*After a pause, laughs.*) So you believe he has deliberately held out? (OSCAR *crosses* D. *to chair* L. C.) For a larger share? (*Leaning forward.*) Well, I *don't* believe it. But I *do* believe that's what *you* want. Am I right, Regina?

REGINA. Oh, I shouldn't like to be too definite. (OSCAR *sits chair* L. C. *To* BEN.) But I *could* say that I wouldn't like to persuade Horace unless he did get a larger share. I must look after his interests. It seems only natural ——

OSCAR. And where would the larger share come from?

REGINA. I don't know. That's not my business. (*Giggles.*) But perhaps it could come off your share, Oscar. (REGINA *and* BEN *laugh.*)

OSCAR. (*Rises and wheels furiously on both of them as they laugh.*) What kind of talk is this?

BEN. I haven't said a thing.

OSCAR. (*Crosses to table* R. *To* REGINA.) *You* are talking very big tonight.

REGINA. (*Stops laughing.*) Am I? Well, you should know me well enough to know that I wouldn't be asking for things I didn't think I could get.

OSCAR. Listen. I don't believe you can even get Horace to come home, much less get money from him or talk quite so big about what you want.

REGINA. Oh, I can get him home.

OSCAR. Then why haven't you?

REGINA. I thought I should fight his battles for him, before he came home. Horace is a very sick man. And even if *you* don't care how sick he is, I do.

BEN. Stop this foolish squabbling. (OSCAR *turns, crosses* L. C.) How can you get him home?

REGINA. I will send Alexandra to Baltimore. She will ask him to come home. She will say that she *wants* him to come home, and that *I* want him to come home.

BIRDIE. (*Suddenly.*) Well, of course she wants him here, but he's sick and maybe he's happy where he is.

REGINA. (*As if she had not heard* BIRDIE, *to* BEN.) You agree that he will come home if she asks him to, if she says that I miss him and want him ——

BEN. (*Looks at her, smiles.*) I admire you, Regina. And I agree. That's settled now, and —— (*Starts to rise.*)

REGINA. (*Quickly stopping him.*) But before she brings him home, I want to know what he's going to get.

BEN. What do you want?

REGINA. Twice what you offered.

BEN. Well, you won't get it.

OSCAR. (*To* REGINA.) I think you've gone crazy.

REGINA. I don't want to fight, Ben ——

BEN. I don't either. You won't get it. There isn't any chance of that. (*Roguishly.*) You're holding us up, and that's not pretty, Regina, not pretty. (*Holds up his hand as he sees she is about to speak.*) But we need you, and I don't want to fight. Here's what I'll do: I'll give Horace forty per cent, instead of the thirty-three and a third he really should get. I'll do that provided he is home and his money is up within two weeks. How's that?

REGINA. All right.

22

OSCAR. (*Crossing* C. *to* BEN.) I've asked before: **Where is this extra share coming from?**

BEN. (*Pleasantly.*) From you. From your share.

OSCAR. (*Furiously. Crosses* R. *to table* R.) From me, is it? That's just fine and dandy. That's my reward. For thirty-five years I've worked my hands to the bone for you. For thirty-five years I've done all the things you didn't want to do. And this is what I ——

BEN. (*Turns slowly to look at* OSCAR. OSCAR *breaks off.*) My, my. I am being attacked tonight on all sides. First by my sister, then by my brother. And I ain't a man who likes being attacked. I can't believe that God wants the strong to parade their strength, but I don't mind doing it, if it's got to be done. (OSCAR *turns, crosses to above chair* L. C., *facing* L. *Leans back in his chair.*) You ought to take these things better, Oscar. I've made you money in the past. I'm going to make you more money now. You'll be a very rich man. What's the difference to any of us if a little more goes here, a little less goes there—it's all in the family. And it will stay in the family. (ADDIE *enters, begins to gather the glasses from table* U. C. OSCAR *turns to* BEN.) So my money will go to Alexandra and Leo. They may even marry some day and —— (ADDIE *looks at* BEN, *then crosses to table* R., *picks up glasses, then crosses to table* U. C., *picks up tray and exits* L.)

BIRDIE. (*Rising.*) Marry—Zan and Leo ——

OSCAR. (*Carefully—crossing* D. *to chair* L. C.) That would make a great difference in my feelings. If they married. (*Sits chair* L. C. BIRDIE *sits chair* U. C.)

BEN. Yes, that's what I mean. Of course it would make a difference.

OSCAR. (*Carefully.*) Is that what *you* mean, Regina?

REGINA. Oh, it's too far away. We'll talk about it in a few years.

OSCAR. I want to talk about it now.

BEN. (*Nods.*) Naturally.

REGINA. There's a lot of things to consider. They are first cousins, and ——

OSCAR. That isn't unusual. Our grandmother and grandfather were first cousins.

REGINA. (*Giggles.*) And look at us. (BEN *giggles.*)

OSCAR. (*Angrily—rises, crosses* D. L.) You're both being very gay with my money. (OSCAR *pacing front piano.*)

BEN. (*Sighs.*) These quarrels. I dislike them so. (*Leans forward to*

23

REGINA. OSCAR *stops walking at table* L. *Listens.*) A **marriage** might be a very wise arrangement, for several reasons. And then, Oscar has given up something for you. You should try to manage something for him.

REGINA. I haven't said I was opposed to it. But Leo is a wild boy. There were those times when he took a little money from the bank and ——

OSCAR. (*A step in.*) That's all past history ——

REGINA. Oh, I know. And I know all young men are wild. I'm only mentioning it to show you that there are considerations ——

BEN. (*Irritated that she does not understand he is trying to keep* OSCAR *quiet.*) All right, so there are. But please assure Oscar that you will think about it very seriously.

REGINA. (*Smiles, nods.*) Very well. I assure Oscar that I will think about it seriously.

OSCAR. (*Sharply.*) That is not an answer.

REGINA. My, (*Rises.*) you're in a bad humor and you shall put me in one. (*Crossing to* C.) I have said all that I am willing to say now. After all, Horace has to give his consent, too.

OSCAR. Horace will do what you tell him to.

REGINA. Yes, I think he will.

OSCAR. (*A step to her.*) And I have your word that you will try to ——

REGINA. (*Patiently. Crosses to him.*) Yes, Oscar. You have my word that I will think about it. Now do leave me alone. (*There is the sound of* ALEXANDRA *and* LEO *opening and closing front door.*)

BIRDIE. (*Rising.*) I —— Alexandra is only seventeen. She ——

REGINA. (*Calling. Crossing in to hall.*) Alexandra? Are you back? (BIRDIE *sits.*)

ALEXANDRA. Yes, Mama.

LEO. (*Comes into room. Crossing* D. L.) Mr. Marshall got off safe and sound. Weren't those fine clothes he had? You can always spot clothes made in a good place. Look like maybe they were done in England. (REGINA *and* ALEXANDRA *enter room.*) Lots of men in the North send all the way to England for their stuff.

BEN. (*To* LEO.) Were you careful driving the horses?

LEO. (*Turns to* BEN.) Oh, yes, sir. I was. (ALEXANDRA *has come in on* BEN's *question, hears answer, looks angrily at* LEO.)

24

ALEXANDRA. (*Crosses to* BIRDIE.) It's a lovely night. You should have come, Aunt Birdie.

REGINA. Were you gracious to Mr. Marshall?

ALEXANDRA. I think so, Mama. I liked him. (LEO *crosses to settee* L.—*sits.*)

REGINA. Good. And now I have great news for you. (ADDIE *enters* L. *with tray with water pitcher and glasses. Crosses to table* U. C. ALEXANDRA *crosses to* REGINA.) You are going to Baltimore in the morning to bring your father home.

ALEXANDRA. (*Gasps, then delighted.*) Me? Papa said I should come? That must mean —— (*Turns to* ADDIE.) Addie, he must be well. (*Crosses to* ADDIE.) Think of it, he'll be back home again. We'll *bring* him home.

REGINA. You are going alone, Alexandra. (*Sits sofa* R.)

ADDIE. (ALEXANDRA *has turned in surprise.*) Going alone? Going by herself? (*Crosses to above table* R.) A child that age! Mr. Horace ain't going to like Zan traipsing up there by herself.

REGINA. (*Sharply.*) Go upstairs and lay out Alexandra's things.

ADDIE. He'd expect me to be along ——

REGINA. I'll be up in a few minutes to tell you what to pack. (ADDIE *slowly begins to climb steps. To* ALEXANDRA.) I should think you'd like going alone. At your age it certainly would have delighted me. You're a strange girl, Alexandra. Addie has babied you so much.

ALEXANDRA. I only thought it would be more fun if Addie and I went together.

BIRDIE. (*Timidly.*) Maybe I could go with her, Regina. I'd really like to.

REGINA. She is going alone. She is getting old enough to take some responsibilities.

OSCAR. She'd better learn now. She's almost old enough to get married. (*Jovially, to* LEO, *slapping him on shoulder.*) Eh, son?

LEO. Huh?

OSCAR. (*Annoyed with* LEO *for not understanding.*) Old enough to get married, you're thinking, eh?

LEO. Oh, yes, sir. (*Feebly.*) Lots of girls get married at Zan's age. Look at Mary Prester and Johanna and ——

REGINA. Well, she's not getting married tomorrow. But she is going to Baltimore tomorrow, so let's talk about *that*. (OSCAR *turns away*

25

—crosses U. L. *To* ALEXANDRA.) You'll be glad to have Papa home again.

ALEXANDRA. I wanted to go before, Mama. You remember that. (*Crosses* R. C.) But you said *you* couldn't go, and that *I* couldn't go alone.

REGINA. I've changed my mind. (*Too casually.*) You're to tell Papa how much you missed him, and that he must come home now—for your sake. Tell him that you *need* him home.

ALEXANDRA. (*Crosses to above table* R.) Need him home? I don't understand.

REGINA. There is nothing for you to understand. You are simply to say what I have told you.

BIRDIE. (*Rises, a step* D. *to* REGINA.) He may be too sick. She couldn't do that ——

ALEXANDRA. Yes. He may be too sick to travel. I couldn't make him think he had to come home for me, if he is too sick to ——

REGINA. (*Looks at her, sharply, challengingly.*) You couldn't do what I tell you to do, Alexandra?

ALEXANDRA. (*Looks at her, quietly.*) No. I couldn't. If I thought it would hurt him.

REGINA. (*After a second's silence, smiles pleasantly.*) But you are doing this for Papa's own good. (*Takes* ALEXANDRA'S *hand.*) You must let me be the judge of his condition. It's the best possible cure for him to come home and be taken care of here. He mustn't stay there any longer and listen to those alarmist doctors. You are doing this entirely for his sake. Tell your Papa that I want him to come home, that I miss him very much.

ALEXANDRA. (*Slowly.*) Yes, Mama.

REGINA. (*To the rest. Rises.*) I must go and start getting Alexandra ready now. (*Crosses* U. C. *to stairs.*) Why don't you all go home?

BEN. (*Rises.*) I'll attend to the railroad ticket. One of the boys will bring it over. (*Crosses* U. R. *back of sofa.*) Good night, everybody. Have a nice trip, Alexandra. The food on the train is very good. The celery is so crisp. Have a good time and act like a little lady. (*He exits.*)

REGINA. (*On landing.*) Good night, Ben. Good night, Oscar —— (*Playfully.*) Don't be so glum, Oscar. It makes you look as if you had chronic indigestion. (*He does not answer.*)

BIRDIE. Good night, Regina.

REGINA. Good night, Birdie. (*Exit upstairs.*)

OSCAR. (*Starts for hall, to* BIRDIE *and* LEO.) Come along.

LEO. (*As he crosses* U. R. *To* ALEXANDRA.) Imagine your not wanting to go! What a little fool you are. (ALEXANDRA *crosses* D. L.) Wish it were me. What I could do in a place like Baltimore!

ALEXANDRA. (*Angrily, looking away from him.*) Mind your business. I can guess the kind of things *you* could do.

LEO. (*Laughs.*) Oh, no, you couldn't. (*He exits.*)

REGINA. (*Calling from top of stairs.*) Come on, Alexandra.

BIRDIE. (*Quickly, crossing* D. L. *to* ALEXANDRA, *softly.*) Zan.

ALEXANDRA. (*Quietly.*) I don't understand about my going, Aunt Birdie. (*Shrugs.*) But anyway, Papa will be home again. (*Pats* BIRDIE'S *arm.*) Don't worry about me. I can take care of myself. Really I can.

BIRDIE. (*Shakes her head, softly.*) That's not what I'm worried about, Zan ——

ALEXANDRA. (*Comes close to her.*) What's the matter?

BIRDIE. It's about Leo ——

ALEXANDRA. (*Whispering.*) He beat the horses. That's why we were late getting back. We had to wait until they cooled off. He always beats the horses as if ——

BIRDIE. (*Whispering frantically, holding* ALEXANDRA'S *hands.*) He's my son. My own son. But you are more to me—more to me than my own child. I love you more than anybody else ——

ALEXANDRA. Don't worry about the horses. I'm sorry I told you.

BIRDIE. (*Her voice rising.*) I am not worrying about the horses. I am worrying about you. You are not going to marry Leo. I am not going to let them do that to you ——

ALEXANDRA. Marry? To Leo? (*Laughs.*) I wouldn't marry, Aunt Birdie. I've never even thought about it ——

BIRDIE. Hush! But they have thought about it. (*Wildly.*) Zan, I couldn't stand to think about such a thing. You and —— (OSCAR *has come into doorway on* ALEXANDRA'S *speech. He is standing quietly, listening.*)

ALEXANDRA. (*Laughs.*) But I'm not going to marry. And I'm certainly not going to marry Leo. (OSCAR *takes one step into room.*)

BIRDIE. Don't you understand? They'll make you. They'll make you ——

ALEXANDRA. (*Takes* BIRDIE'S *hands, quietly, firmly.*) That's foolish, Aunt Birdie. I'm grown now. Nobody can make me do anything.

BIRDIE. I just couldn't stand ——

OSCAR. (*Sharply.*) Birdie. (BIRDIE *looks up, draws quickly away from* ALEXANDRA. *She stands rigid, fearful. Quietly.*) Birdie, get your hat and coat.

ADDIE. (*Unseen, calls from upstairs hallway.*) Come on, baby. Your Mama's waiting for you, and she ain't nobody to keep waiting.

ALEXANDRA. All right. (*Then softly, embracing* BIRDIE.) Good night, Aunt Birdie. (*Crosses upstairs. As she passes* OSCAR.) Good night, Uncle Oscar. (BIRDIE *begins to move slowly towards door as* ALEXANDRA *climbs the stairs.* ALEXANDRA *is almost out of view when* BIRDIE *reaches* OSCAR *in doorway. As* BIRDIE *quickly attempts to pass him, he slaps her hard, across the face.* BIRDIE *cries out, puts her hand to her face. On the cry,* ALEXANDRA *turns, begins to run down the stairs.*) Aunt Birdie! What happened? What happened? I ——

BIRDIE. (*Softly, without turning.*) Nothing, darling. Nothing happened. (*Quickly, as if anxious to keep* ALEXANDRA *from coming close.*) Now go to bed. (OSCAR *exits.*) Nothing happened. (*Turns to* ALEXANDRA, *who is holding her hand.*) I only—I only twisted my ankle. (*She goes out.* ALEXANDRA *stands on stairs looking after her as if she were puzzled and frightened.*)

MEDIUM CURTAIN

ACT II

AT RISE: *The light comes from the open shutter of R. window, the other shutters are tightly closed.* ADDIE *is standing at window, looking out. Near dining-room doors are brooms, mops, rags, etc. After a second* OSCAR *comes into entrance hall, looks in the room, shivers, decides not to takes his hat and coat off, comes into the room. At the sound of door,* ADDIE *turns to see who has come in.*

ADDIE. (*Without interest.*) Oh, it's you, Mr. Oscar. (ADDIE *turns back to window, closes windows.*)

OSCAR. What is this? It's not night. (*Crosses to above sofa* R.) What's the matter here? (*Shivers.* ADDIE *crosses to* U. *windows.*) Fine thing at this time of the morning. Blinds all closed. (ADDIE *begins to open shutters. The room lights up.*) Where's Miss Regina? It's cold in here. (*He crosses* C.)

ADDIE. Miss Regina ain't down yet.

OSCAR. She had any word?

ADDIE. (*Wearily, crossing* D. *to chair* D. C., *picks up feather duster.*) No, sir.

OSCAR. (*Crossing to settee* L.) Wouldn't you think a girl that age could get on a train at one place and have sense enough to get off at another? (*He sits settee.*)

ADDIE. (*At chair* D. R.) Something must have happened. (*Crosses to sofa* R. *for broom.*) If Zan say she was coming last night, she's coming last night. Unless something happened. (*Crosses* U. L.) Sure fire disgrace to let a baby like that go all that way alone to bring home a sick man without ——

OSCAR. You do a lot of judging around here, Addie, eh? Judging of your white folks, I mean.

ADDIE. (*Looks at him, sighs.*) I'm tired. I been up all night watching for them.

REGINA. (*Who cannot be seen. Speaking from upstairs hall.*) Who's downstairs, Addie? (*She appears in a dressing gown, peers*

29

down from landing. ADDIE *picks up carpet sweeper, dustpan and brush, standing* R. *of dining-room doors, exits* L.) Oh, it's you, Oscar. What are you doing here so early? I haven't been down yet. I'm not finished dressing.

OSCAR. (*Speaking up to her.*) You had any word from them?

REGINA. No.

OSCAR. Then something certainly has happened. People don't just say they are arriving on Thursday night, and they haven't come by Friday morning.

REGINA. Oh, nothing has happened. Alexandra just hasn't got sense enough to send a message.

OSCAR. (*Rises, crosses* U. C.) If nothing's happened, then why aren't they here?

REGINA. You asked me that ten times last night. My, you do fret so, Oscar. Anything might have happened. They may have missed connections in Atlanta, the train may have been delayed—oh, a hundred things could have kept them.

OSCAR. (*Crosses* R.) Where's Ben?

REGINA. (*As she disappears up stairs.*) Where should he be? At home, probably. Really, Oscar, I don't tuck him in his bed and I don't take him out of it. Have some coffee and don't worry so much.

OSCAR. Have some coffee? (*Crosses* U. C.) There isn't any coffee. (*Looks at his watch, shakes his head. After a second* CAL *enters with a large silver tray, coffee urn, six small cups, newspaper. He puts tray on table* U. C., *begins to set out cups.*) Oh, there you are. (*Crosses* D. C.) Is everything in this house always late? (*Takes off coat and hat.*)

CAL. (*Looks at him surprised.*) You ain't out shooting this morning, Mr. Oscar?

OSCAR. (*Places coat and hat on chair* U. C.) First day I missed since I had a head cold. First day I missed in eight years. (*Crosses* D. L., *sits on settee.*)

CAL. Yes, sir. I bet you. Simon he say you had a mighty good day yesterday morning. That's what Simon say. (*Brings* OSCAR *small coffee and newspaper.*)

OSCAR. Pretty good, pretty good. (*Opens newspaper.*)

CAL. (*Laughs, slyly, puts coffee cup on table* L. *of settee, moves table toward* OSCAR.) Bet you got enough bob-white and squirrel to give every nigger in town a Jesus-party. Most of 'em ain't had no meat since the cotton picking was over. Bet they'd give anything for a little piece of that meat ——

OSCAR. (*Turns his head to look at* CAL.) Cal, if I catch a nigger in this town going shooting, you know what's going to happen. (LEO *enters.*)

CAL. (*Hastily steps back.*) Yes, sir, Mr. Oscar. I didn't say nothing about nothing. It was Simon who told me and —— Morning, Mr. Leo. You gentlemen having your breakfast with us here?

LEO. (*Comes immediately to* OSCAR.) The boys in the bank don't know a thing. They haven't had any message. (CAL *waits for answer, gets none, shrugs, moves to door* L., *looks back at them, exits.*)

OSCAR. (*Peers at* LEO.) What you doing here, son?

LEO. You told me to find out if the boys at the bank had any message from Uncle Horace or Zan ——

OSCAR. I told you if they had a message to bring it here. I told you that if they didn't have a message to stay at the bank and do your work.

LEO. Oh, I guess I misunderstood.

OSCAR. You didn't misunderstand. You just were looking for any excuse to take an hour off. (LEO *crosses to table* U. C., *pours coffee.*) You got to stop that kind of thing. You got to start settling down. You going to be a married man one of these days.

LEO. Yes, sir.

OSCAR. You also got to stop with that woman in Mobile. (*As* LEO *is about to speak, he puts up a hand.* LEO *turns back for sugar.*) You're young and I haven't got no objections to outside women. That is, I haven't got no objections so long as they don't interfere with serious things. Outside women are all right in their place, but *now* isn't their place! You got to realize that.

LEO. (*Nods.*) Yes, sir. I'll tell her. She'll act all right about it. (*He drinks his coffee.*)

OSCAR. Also, you got to start working harder at the bank. You got to convince your Uncle Horace you going to make a fit husband for Alexandra.

LEO. (*Crossing* D. *to back of settee* L.) What do you think has happened to them? Supposed to be here last night —— (*Laughs —crosses to* C.) Bet you Uncle Ben's mighty worried. Seventy-five thousand dollars worried.

OSCAR. (*Smiles happily.*) Ought to be worried. Damn well ought to be. First he don't answer the letters, then he don't come home —— (*Giggles.*)

LEO. (*Crosses L. to chair L. C.*) What will happen if Uncle Horace don't come home or don't ——?

OSCAR. Or don't put up the money? Oh, we'll get it from outside. Easy enough.

LEO. (*Surprised.*) But *you* don't want outsiders. (*Sits chair L. C.*)

OSCAR. What do I care who gets my share? I been shaved already. Serve Ben right if he had to give away some of his.

LEO. Damn shame what they did to you. (*Picks up cup to drink.*)

OSCAR. (*Looking up stairs.*) Don't talk so loud. (LEO *starts to speak.*) Don't you worry. When I die, you'll have as much as the rest. You might have yours *and* Alexandra's. I'm not so easily licked.

LEO. (*Smoothly.*) I wasn't thinking of myself, Papa ——

OSCAR. Well, you should be, you should be. It's every man's duty to think of himself.

LEO. (*Turns to* OSCAR.) You think Uncle Horace don't want to go in on this?

OSCAR. (*Giggles.*) That's my hunch. (LEO *drinks.*) He hasn't showed any signs of loving it yet. (LEO *looks at empty cup.*)

LEO. (*Laughs—turns front.*) But he hasn't listened to Aunt Regina yet, either. Oh, he'll go along. It's too good a thing. (*Rises.*) Why wouldn't he want to? (*Crosses U. C. to pour another coffee.*) He's got plenty and plenty to invest with. He don't even have to sell anything. Eighty-eight thousand worth of Union Pacific bonds sitting right in his safe deposit box. All he's got to do is open the box. (*Turns front.*)

OSCAR. (*After a pause. Looks at his watch.*) Mighty late breakfast in this fancy house. (LEO *drinks.*) Yes, he's had those bonds for fifteen years. Bought them when they were low and just locked them up.

LEO. (*Nods—steps D. C.*) Yeah. Just has to open the box and take them out. That's all. Easy as easy can be. (*Laughs.*) The things in that box! There's all those bonds, looking mighty fine. (OSCAR *slowly puts down his newspaper and turns to* LEO.) Then right next to them is a baby shoe of Zan's and a cheap old cameo on a string, and, *and*—nobody'd believe this—a piece of an old violin. Not even a whole violin. Just a piece of an old thing, a piece of a violin.

32

OSCAR. (*Very softly, as if he were trying to control his voice—looking at* LEO.) A piece of a violin! What do you think of that!

LEO. Yes, siree. (*Crossing* R. *to table, puts cup down.*) A lot of other crazy things, too. (*Turns to* OSCAR *who is staring at him.*) A poem, I guess it is, signed with his mother's name, and two old school books with notes and —— (LEO *catches* OSCAR'S *look. His voice trails off. He turns his head away.*)

OSCAR. (*Very softly.*) How do you know what's in the box, son?

LEO. (*Stops, draws back, frightened, realizing what he has said. Then after a second, he manages to speak.*) Oh, well, well—er. (*Crossing* L. *to chair* L. C.) Well, one of the boys, sir. It was one of the boys at the bank. He took old Mander's keys. It was Joe Horns. He just up and took Manders' keys and, and—well, took the box out. (*Quickly.*) Then they all asked me if I wanted to see, too. So I looked a little, I guess, but then I made them close up the box quick and I told them never ——

OSCAR. (*Looks at him.*) Joe Horns, you say? He opened it?

LEO. Yes, sir, yes, he did. My word of honor. (*Very nervously looking away.*) I suppose that don't excuse me for looking,— (*Looking at* OSCAR.) but I did make him close it up and put the keys back in Manders' drawer ——

OSCAR. (*Leans forward, very softly.*) Tell me the truth, Leo. I am not going to be angry with you. Did you open the box yourself?

LEO. No, sir, I didn't. I told you I didn't. No, I ——

OSCAR. (*Irritated, patient.*) I am not going to be angry with you. (LEO *turns—crosses to table* R. *Watching* LEO *carefully.*) Sometimes a young fellow deserves credit for looking round him to see what's going on. Sometimes that's a good sign in a fellow your age. (LEO *turns head to listen.* OSCAR *rises.*) Many great men have made their fortune with their eyes. (*Crosses to* C.) Did you open the box?

LEO. (*Very puzzled.*) No. I ——

OSCAR. (*Taking a step to him.*) Did you open the box? It may have been—(*Moving to* LEO.) well, it may have been a good thing if you had.

LEO. (*After a long pause.*) I opened it.

OSCAR. (*Quickly.*) Is that the truth? (LEO *nods.*) Does anybody also know that you opened it? Come, Leo, don't be afraid of speaking the truth to me.

33

LEO. No. Nobody knew. Nobody was in the bank when I did it. But ——

OSCAR. Did your Uncle Horace ever know you opened it?

LEO. (*Shakes his head.*) He only looks in it once every six months when he cuts the coupons, and sometimes Mander even does that for him. Uncle Horace don't even have the keys. Mander keeps them for him. Imagine not looking at all that. You can bet if I had the bonds, I'd watch 'em like ——

OSCAR. If you had them. (*Turns front, crossing* R. *to sofa.* LEO *watches him.*) If you had them. Then you could have the share in the mill, you and me. (*Turns to* LEO.) A fine, big share, too. (*Pauses—shrugs.*) Well, a man can't be shot for wanting to see his son get on in the world, can he, boy? (OSCAR *sits on sofa* R.)

LEO. (*Looks up, begins to understand.*) No, he can't! Natural enough. (*Laughs.*) But I haven't got the bonds and Uncle Horace has. And now we can just sit back and wait to be a millionaire.

OSCAR. (*Innocently.*) You think your Uncle Horace likes you well enough to lend *you* the bonds if he decides not to use them himself?

LEO. Papa, it must be that you haven't had your breakfast! (*Laughs loudly.*) Lend me the bonds! My God ——

OSCAR. (*Disappointed.*) No, I suppose not. Just a fancy of mine. A loan for three months, maybe four, easy enough for us to pay it back then. Anyway, this is only April—(*Slowly counting the months on his fingers.*) and if he doesn't look at them until fall, he wouldn't even *miss* them out of the box.

LEO. That's it. He wouldn't even miss them. Ah, well ——

OSCAR. No, sir. Wouldn't even miss them. How could he miss them if he never looks at them? (*Sighs as* LEO *stares at him.*) Well, here we are sitting around waiting for him to come home and invest his money in something he hasn't lifted his hand to get. (LEO *crosses* L. C.) But I can't help thinking he's acting strange. You laugh when I say he could lend you the bonds if he's not going to use them himself. But would it hurt him?

LEO. (*Slowly looking at* OSCAR.) No. No, it wouldn't.

OSCAR. People *ought* to help other people. But that's not always the way it happens. (BEN *enters, hangs his coat and hat on hall tree. Very carefully.*) And so sometimes you got to think of yourself. (*As* LEO *stares at him,* BEN *appears in doorway.*) Morning, Ben.

BEN. (*Coming in, carrying his newspaper. Crosses to chair* R. C.) Fine, sunny morning. Any news from the runaways? (BEN *sits chair* R. C.)

REGINA. (*On landing.*) There's no news or you would have heard it. (*Coming downstairs.*) Quite a convention so early in the morning, aren't you all? (*Goes to coffee urn.*)

OSCAR. You rising mighty late these days. Is that the way they do things in Chicago society?

BEN. (*Looking at his paper.*) Old Carter died up in Senateville. Eighty-one is a good time for us all, eh? What do you think has really happened to Horace, Regina?

REGINA. Nothing.

BEN. (*Too casually, still reading.*) You don't think maybe he never started from Baltimore and never intends to start?

REGINA. (*Irritated—steps* D.) Of course they've started. Didn't I have a letter from Alexandra? What is so strange about people arriving late? (*Crosses* U. *to table—pours coffee.*) He has that cousin in Savannah he's so fond of. He may have stopped to see him. They'll be along today sometime, very flattered that you and Oscar are so worried about them. (*Steps* D.)

BEN. I'm a natural worrier. Especially when I am getting ready to close a business deal and one of my partners remains silent *and* invisible.

REGINA. (*Laughs.*) Oh, is that it? I thought you were worried about Horace's health.

OSCAR. Oh, that too. Who could help but worry? *I'm* worried. This is the first day I haven't shot since my head cold.

REGINA. (*Starts toward dining-room.*) Then you haven't had your breakfast. Come along. (OSCAR *and* LEO *follow her.* BEN *remains seated.*)

BEN. Regina. (*She turns at dining-room door.*) That cousin of Horace's has been dead for years and, in any case, the train does not go through Savannah.

REGINA. (*Laughs. Then continues into dining-room, seats herself, motions to* LEO *and* OSCAR.) Did he die? You're always remembering about people dying. (BEN *rises, leaves newspaper on table, crosses* U. L. *to dining-room.*) Now I intend to eat my breakfast in peace, and read my newspaper. (*Rings bell.*)

BEN. (*Goes toward dining-room as he talks.*) This is second breakfast for me. My first was bad. Celia ain't the cook she used to be.

35

Too old to have taste any more. If she hadn't belonged to Mama, I'd send her off to the country. (CAL *is putting two silver serving dishes on table.* OSCAR *and* LEO *start to eat.* BEN *seats himself.*)

LEO. Uncle Horace will have some tales to tell, I bet. Baltimore is a lively town.

REGINA. (*To* CAL.) The grits isn't hot enough. Take it back.

CAL. Oh, yes'm. (*Calling into kitchen as he exits off dining-room.*) Grits didn't hold the heat. Grits didn't hold the heat.

LEO. When I was at school three of the boys and myself took a train once and went over to Baltimore. It was so big we thought we were in Europe. I was just a kid then ——

REGINA. (*Looks up, helps herself from a dish.*) I find it very pleasant—(ADDIE *enters from* L.) to have breakfast alone. I hate chattering before I've had something hot. (CAL *has come back, closes dining-room doors.*) Do be still, Leo. (ADDIE *comes into room, begins gathering up cups, carries them to the large tray, then quickly she runs into hall. Outside there are sounds of* VOICES *and* PEOPLE *moving about. A few seconds later* ADDIE *appears again in doorway, her arm around the shoulders of* HORACE GIDDENS, *supporting him.* HORACE *is a tall man of about forty-five. He has been good-looking, but now his face is tired and ill. He walks stiffly, as if it were an enormous effort, and carefully, as if he were unsure of his balance.* ADDIE *takes off his overcoat and hangs it on hall tree. She then helps him across to chair* L. C.)

HORACE. (*As they are crossing.*) How are you, Addie? How have you been?

ADDIE. I'm all right, Mr. Horace. I've just been worried about you. (HORACE *sits in chair.* ALEXANDRA *enters. She is flushed and excited, her hat awry, her face dirty. Her arms are full of packages, but she comes quickly to* ADDIE.)

ALEXANDRA. Now don't tell me how worried you were. We couldn't help it and there was no way to send a message.

ADDIE. (*To* HORACE, *begins to take packages from* ALEXANDRA.) Yes, sir, I was mighty worried.

ALEXANDRA. We had to stop in Mobile overnight. Papa—(*Looks at him.*) Papa didn't feel well. The trip was too much for him, and I made him stop and rest —— (*As* ADDIE *takes last package.*) No, don't take that. That's Father's medicine. (*Crosses* D. *to table* R. C. ADDIE *puts the packages on the chair* L. *of table* U. C. *then crosses to* ALEXANDRA.) I'll hold it. It mustn't break. Now, about the stuff

36

outside. Papa must have his wheel chair. I'll get that and the valises —— (ALEXANDRA *starts to go, but* ADDIE *stops her.*)

ADDIE. (*Very happy, holding* ALEXANDRA'S *arms.*) Since when you got to carry your own valises? Since when I ain't old enough to hold a bottle of medicine? (HORACE *coughs. Turns and steps to* HORACE. ALEXANDRA *looks at* HORACE.) You feel all right, Mr. Horace?

HORACE. (*Nods.*) Glad to be sitting down.

ALEXANDRA. (*Opening package of medicine on table* R. C.) He doesn't feel all right. (ADDIE *looks at her, then at* HORACE.) He just says that. The trip was very hard on him, and now he must go right to bed.

ADDIE. (*Looking at him carefully.*) Them fancy doctors, they give you help?

HORACE. They did their best.

LEO. (*In dining-room.*) Papa, can I have your part of the paper?

ALEXANDRA. (*Has become conscious of voices in dining room.*) I bet Mama was worried. I better tell her we're here now. (*She starts for door.*)

HORACE. Zan. (*She stops, steps* D. *to above settee* L.) Not for a minute, dear.

ALEXANDRA. Oh, Papa, you feel bad again. I knew you did. Do you want your medicine?

HORACE. No, I don't feel that way. I'm just tired, darling. Let me rest a little.

ALEXANDRA. Yes, but Mama will be mad if I don't tell her we're here.

ADDIE. They're all in there eating breakfast.

ALEXANDRA. Oh, are they all here? (*Crosses to* ADDIE.) Why do they *always* have to be here? I was hoping Papa wouldn't have to see anybody, that it would be nice for him and quiet.

ADDIE. (*Patting* ALEXANDRA'S *arm.*) Then let your Papa rest for a minute.

HORACE. Addie, I bet your coffee's as good as ever. They don't have such good coffee up North. (*Looks hungrily at urn.*) Is it as good, Addie? (ADDIE *starts for coffee urn.*)

ALEXANDRA. No. (*Step to* ADDIE—*stops her.*) Dr. Reeves said not much coffee. Just now and then. (*Proudly to* ADDIE.) I'm the nurse now, Addie.

ADDIE. You'd be a better one if you didn't look so dirty. (*Taking*

ALEXANDRA to stairs.) Now go and take a bath, Miss Grownup. Change your linens, get out a fresh dress and give your hair a good brushing—go on ——

ALEXANDRA. Will you be all right, Papa?

ADDIE. (Slapping her backside.) Go on.

ALEXANDRA. (On stairs, talks as she goes up.) The pills Papa must take once every four hours. (ADDIE steps into room.) And the bottle only when—only if he feels very bad. (On landing.) Now don't move until I come back and don't talk much and remember about his medicine, Addie ——

ADDIE. Ring for Belle and have her help you and then I'll make you a fresh breakfast.

ALEXANDRA. (As she disappears upstairs.) How's Aunt Birdie? Is she here?

ADDIE. (Crosses D. R. of HORACE.) It ain't right for you to have coffee? It will hurt you?

HORACE. (Slowly.) Nothing can make much difference now. Get me a cup, Addie. (She looks at him, crosses to urn, pours a cup.) Funny. They can't make coffee up North. (ADDIE brings him a cup.) They don't like red paper, either. (He takes cup and gulps it greedily.) God, that's good. You remember how I used to drink it? Ten, twelve cups a day. (Slight laugh as he picks up cup again. He speaks more slowly.) Addie, before I see anybody else, I want to know why Zan came to fetch me home. She's tried to tell me, but she doesn't seem to know herself. (Drinks.)

ADDIE. (Turns away.) I don't know. (Crosses R. to table.) All I know is big things are going on. (To HORACE.) Everybody going to be high-tone rich. Big rich. You too. (Looks away—at table.) All because smoke's going to start out of a building that ain't even up yet. (She angrily creases medicine bottle paper on table.)

HORACE. I've heard about it.

ADDIE. And, er —— (Hesitates—step to him.) And—well, Zan, she going to marry Mr. Leo in a little while.

HORACE. (Looks at her, then very slowly.) What are you talking about?

ADDIE. (Crossing to R. of HORACE.) That's right. That's the talk, God help us.

HORACE. (Angrily.) What's the talk?

ADDIE. I'm telling you. There's going to be a wedding —— (An-

38

grily clenches paper in her hand, turns head away.) Over my dead body there is.

HORACE. (*He hands cup to* ADDIE, *not looking at her. After a second, quietly.*) Go and tell them I'm home.

ADDIE. (*Hesitates.*) Now you ain't to get excited. You're to be in your bed ——

HORACE. Go on, Addie. Go and say I'm back. (ADDIE *takes cup and paper to tray, looking at him as he is rising, then crosses* L. *and opens dining-room doors. He rises with difficulty, stands stiff as if he were in pain, facing dining-room.*)

ADDIE. (*Opens doors, then stands in corner* U. L.) Miss Regina. They're home. They got here —— (*Everybody turns to look at her.*)

BEN. They are?

OSCAR. Good.

LEO. Just now?

REGINA. Horace. (REGINA *quickly rises, runs into room. Others follow her.* REGINA, *warmly.*) Horace! You've finally arrived. (*As she kisses him, the others come forward, all talking together.*)

BEN. (*In doorway, carrying a napkin.*) Well, sir, you had us all mighty worried. (*He steps forward. They shake hands.* ADDIE *watches them, then exits* L.)

OSCAR. (*Crossing to above settee.*) You're a sight for sore eyes.

HORACE. Hello, Ben. (BEN *crosses* R. C. LEO *enters eating biscuit.*)

OSCAR. And how you feel? Tip-top, I bet, because that's the way you're looking.

HORACE. (*Coldly, irritated with* OSCAR'S *lie.*) Hello, Oscar. Hello, Leo. (LEO *steps* D., *extends hand.*) How are you?

LEO. (*Shaking hands.*) I'm fine, sir. But a lot better now that you're back.

REGINA. (*Step to* HORACE.) Now sit down. (LEO *backs away* D. L. *as* HORACE *sits.*) What did happen to you and where's Alexandra? I am so excited about seeing you that I almost forgot about her.

HORACE. I didn't feel good, a little weak, I guess, and we stopped overnight to rest. Zan's upstairs washing off the train dirt.

REGINA. (*Crossing above* HORACE, *to his* L.) Oh, I am so sorry the trip was hard on you. I didn't think that ——

HORACE. (*Sarcastically, looking around at them.*) Well, it's just as if I had never been away. All of you here ——

BEN. Waiting to welcome you home. (BIRDIE *bursts in. She is wearing a flannel kimono and her face is flushed and excited.* BEN *crosses* D. R. *to mantel.*)

BIRDIE. (*Runs to him, kisses him.*) Horace!

HORACE. (*Warmly, pressing her arm.*) I was just wondering where you were, Birdie.

BIRDIE. (*Excited.*) Oh, I would have been here. I didn't know you were back until Simon said he saw the buggy —— (*She draws back to look at him. Her face sobers.*) Oh, you don't look well, Horace. No you don't.

REGINA. (*Laughs.*) Birdie, what a thing to say ——

HORACE. (*Looking at* OSCAR.) Oscar thinks I look very well.

OSCAR. (*Annoyed. Turns on* LEO.) Don't stand there holding that biscuit in your hand. (*Crosses* R. *to above chair* R. C.)

LEO. Oh. Well, I'll just finish my breakfast, Uncle Horace, and then I'll give you all the news about the bank —— (*He exits into dining-room, taking newspaper from settee.*)

OSCAR. (*Comes to* R. *of* BIRDIE.) And what is that costume you have on?

BIRDIE. (*Is looking at* HORACE.) Now that you're home, you'll feel better. Plenty of good rest and we'll take such fine care of you —— (*Stops.*) But where is Zan? (HORACE *motions to stair-case.*) I missed her so much.

OSCAR. I asked you what is that strange costume you're parading around in?

BIRDIE. (*Nervously, backing toward stairs.*) Me? (*Looks at costume—drops* HORACE'S *hand.* OSCAR *crosses* U. R.) Oh! It's my wrapper. I was so excited about Horace I just rushed out of the house ——

OSCAR. Did you come across the square dressed that way? My dear Birdie, I ——

HORACE. (*To* REGINA, *wearily.*) Yes, it's just like old times.

REGINA. (*Quickly to* OSCAR.) Now no fights. This is a holiday.

BIRDIE. (*Runs quickly upstairs.*) Zan! Zannie!

OSCAR. Birdie! (*She stops.*)

BIRDIE. Tell Zan I'll be back in a little while. (*Exits door* R.)

REGINA. (*To* OSCAR *and* BEN.) Why don't you go finish your break-fast—(*Looks at* OSCAR. *He looks at* BEN, *then crosses into dining-room.* REGINA *crosses* D. C.) and let Horace rest for a minute?

BEN. (*Crossing to dining-room.* REGINA *crosses* D. R.) Never leave a meal unfinished. There are too many poor people who need the food. Mighty glad to see you home, Horace. Fine to have you back. Fine to have you back.

OSCAR. (*To* LEO *as* BEN *is closing dining-room doors.*) Your mother has gone crazy. Running around the streets like a woman —— (*The moment* REGINA *and* HORACE *are alone, they become awkward and self-conscious.*)

REGINA. (*Laughs awkwardly.*) Well. Here we are. It's been a long time. (HORACE *smiles.*) Five months. You know, Horace, I wanted to come and be with you in the hospital, but I didn't know where my duty was. Here, or with you. But you know how much I *wanted* to come.

HORACE. That's kind of you, Regina. There was no need to come.

REGINA. Oh, but there was. Five months lying there all by yourself, no kin-folk, no friends. Don't try to tell me you didn't have a bad time of it.

HORACE. I didn't have a bad time. (*As she shakes her head, he becomes insistent.*) No, I didn't, Regina. Oh, at first when I— when I heard the news about myself—but after I got used to that, I liked it there.

REGINA. You *liked* it? (*Coldly.*) Isn't that strange! You liked it so well you didn't want to come home?

HORACE. That's not the way to put it. (*Then, kindly, as he sees her turn her head away.*) But there I was and I got kind of used to it, kind of to like lying there and thinking. (*Smiles.*) I never had much time to think before. And time's become valuable to me.

REGINA. It sounds almost like a holiday. (*Takes a step* R.)

HORACE. (*Laughs.*) It was, sort of. The first holiday I've had since I was a little kid.

REGINA. And here I was thinking you were in pain and ——

HORACE. (*Quietly.*) I *was* in pain.

REGINA. And instead you were having a holiday! (*She sits chair* R. C.) A holiday of thinking. Couldn't you have done that here?

HORACE. I wanted to do it before I came here. I was thinking about us.

REGINA. About us? About you and me? Thinking about you and me after all these years? (*Unpleasantly. Rises, crosses* D. R.) You shall tell me everything you thought—some day.

HORACE. (*There is silence for a minute.*) Regina. (*She turns to him.*) Why did you send Zan to Baltimore?

REGINA. Why? Because I wanted you home. (*Crossing to him.*) You can't make anything suspicious out of that, can you?

HORACE. I didn't mean to make anything suspicious about it. (*Hesitantly, taking her hand.*) Zan said you wanted me to come home. I was so pleased at that and touched, it made me feel good.

REGINA. (*Taking away her hand, turns.*) Touched that I should want you home?

HORACE. (*Sighs.*) I'm saying all the wrong things, as usual. Let's try to get along better. There isn't so much more time. Regina, what's all this crazy talk I've been hearing about Zan and Leo? (*Slight laugh.*) Zan and Leo marrying?

REGINA. (*Turning to him, sharply.*) Who gossips so much around here?

HORACE. (*Shocked.*) Regina!

REGINA. (*Annoyed, anxious to quiet him, a step to him.*) It's some foolishness that Oscar thought up. I'll explain later. I have no intention of allowing any such arrangement. It was simply a way of keeping Oscar quiet in all this business I've been writing you about ——

HORACE. (*Carefully.*) What has Zan to do with any business of Oscar's? Whatever it is, you had better put it out of Oscar's head immediately. You know what I think of Leo.

REGINA. But there's no need to talk about it now.

HORACE. There is no need to talk about it ever. Not as long as I live. (REGINA *turns, crosses* R. HORACE *stops, slowly, turns to look at her.*) As long as I live. I've been in a hospital for five months. Yet since I've been here you have not once asked me about— about my health. (*Then gently.*) Well, I suppose they've written you. I can't live very long.

REGINA. (*Coldly.*) I've never understood why people have to talk about this kind of thing. (*Crosses* U. R.)

HORACE. (*A silence. Then he looks up at her, his face cold.*) You misunderstand. (REGINA *pacing* U. R. C.) I don't intend to gossip about my sickness. I thought it was only fair to tell you. I was not asking for your sympathy.

REGINA. (*Sharply, turns to him.*) What do the doctors think caused your bad heart?

HORACE. What do you mean?

REGINA. (R. *of* HORACE.) They didn't think it possible, did they, that your fancy women may have ——?

HORACE. (Smiles, unpleasantly.) Caused my heart to be bad? I don't think that's the best scientific theory. You don't catch heart trouble in bed.

REGINA. (Angrily.) I didn't think you did. I only thought you might catch a bad conscience—in bed, as you say. (Crosses D. R.)

HORACE. I didn't tell them about my bad conscience. Or about my fancy women. Nor did I tell them that my wife has not wanted me in bed with her for —— (Sharply.) How long is it, Regina? (REGINA turns to him.) Ten years? Did you bring me home for this, to make me feel guilty again? That means you want something. But you'll not make me feel guilty any more. My "thinking" has made a difference.

REGINA. I see that it has.

BEN. (In dining-room.) Put down that paper, Leo.

REGINA. (She looks toward dining-room door. Then comes to him, her manner warm and friendly.) It's foolish for us to fight this way. I didn't mean to be unpleasant. I was stupid.

HORACE. (Wearily.) God knows I didn't either. I came home wanting so much not to fight, and then all of a sudden there we were. I got hurt and ——

REGINA. (Hastily.) It's all my fault. I didn't ask about—your illness because I didn't want to remind you of it. Anyway I never believe doctors when they talk about—(Brightly.) when they talk like that.

HORACE. (Not looking at her.) Well, we'll try our best with each other. (He rises, starts for stairs. He gets as far as chair R. C. when REGINA stops him.)

REGINA. (Quickly, crossing with him.) I'll try. Honestly, I will. Horace, (He stops, turns to her.) Horace, I know you're tired but, but—couldn't you stay down here a few minutes longer? I want Ben to tell you something.

HORACE. Tomorrow.

REGINA. I'd like to now. It's very important to me. It's very important to all of us. (Gaily, as she moves toward dining-room.) Important to your beloved daughter. She'll be a very great heiress ——

HORACE. Will she? That's nice.

REGINA. (Opens doors.) Ben, are you finished breakfast?

HORACE. Is this the mill business I've had so many letters about?

REGINA. (To BEN.) Horace would like to talk to you now.

HORACE. Horace would not like to talk to you now. I am very tired, Regina —— (*He starts.*)

REGINA. (*Comes to him and stops him.*) Please. You've said we'll try our best with each other. I'll try. Really, I will. But please do this for me now. (*Urging him into chair R. C.*) You will see what I've done while you've been away. How I watched your interests. (*Laughs gaily.*) And I've done very well, too. But things can't be delayed any longer. Everything must be settled this week —— (HORACE *crosses—sits chair R. C.* REGINA *crosses to* BEN *who is entering. Brings him C.* OSCAR *has stayed in the dining-room, his head turned to watch them.* LEO *is pretending to read newspaper.*) Now you must tell Horace all about it. Only be quick because he is very tired and must go to bed. (HORACE *is looking up at her as if he finally understood. His face hardens as she speaks.*) But I think your news will be better for him than all the medicine in the world.

BEN. (*Who is looking at* HORACE.) It could wait. Horace may not feel like talking today.

REGINA. What an old faker you are! You know it can't wait. You know it must be finished this week. (*Crosses D. R.*) You've been just as anxious for Horace to get here as I've been.

BEN. (*Very jovial.*) I suppose I have been. And why not? Horace has done Hubbard Sons many a good turn. Why shouldn't I be anxious to help him now?

REGINA. (*Laughs.*) Help him! Help him when you need him, that's what you mean. (*Sits sofa R.*)

BEN. What a woman you married, Horace! (*Laughs awkwardly when* HORACE *does not answer.*) Well, then I'll make it quick. You know what I've been telling you for years. How I've always said that every one of us little Southern business men had great things —(*Extends his arm, moves his fingers.*) right beyond our finger tips. It's been my dream: my dream to make those fingers grow longer. I'm a lucky man, Horace, a lucky man. To dream and to live to get what you've dreamed of. That's my idea of a lucky man. (*Looks at his fingers as his arm drops slowly.*) For thirty years I've cried, bring the cotton mills to the cotton! (HORACE *opens medicine bottle, pours dose into spoon.*) Well, finally I got up nerve to go to the Marshall Company in Chicago.

HORACE. (*Has finally taken his eyes from* REGINA.) I know all this. (*He takes medicine.* REGINA *rises, a step to him.*)

BEN. Can I get you something?

HORACE. Some water, please.

REGINA. (*Turns quickly.*) Oh, I'm sorry. Let me. (*Crosses to tray on table* U. C., *brings him glass. He drinks as they wait in silence.*) You feel all right now?

HORACE. Yes. You wrote me. I know all that. (OSCAR *rises—crosses to dining-room doors.*)

REGINA. (*Triumphantly.*) But you don't know that in the last few days Ben has agreed to give us—you, I mean—a much larger share.

HORACE. Really? That's very generous of him. (OSCAR *crosses* D. *to above settee* L.)

BEN. (*Laughs.*) It wasn't so generous of me; it was smart of Regina.

REGINA. (*As if she were signalling* HORACE.) I explained to Ben that perhaps you hadn't answered his letters because you didn't think he was offering you enough, and that the time was getting short and you could guess how much he needed you ——

HORACE. (*Smiles at her—nods.*) And I could guess that he wants to keep control in the family?

REGINA. (*To* BEN, *triumphantly.*) Exactly. (*To* HORACE.) So I did a little bargaining for you and convinced my brothers they weren't the only Hubbards who had a business sense. (*Crosses* D. *to front sofa.*)

HORACE. Did you have to convince them of that? How little people know about each other! (OSCAR *crosses* D. L. *slowly. Laughs.*) But you'll know better about Regina next time, eh, Ben? (BEN, REGINA, HORACE *laugh together.* OSCAR'S *face is angry.*) Now let's see. We're getting a bigger share. (*Looking at* OSCAR.) Who's getting less?

BEN. Oscar.

HORACE. Well, Oscar, you've grown very unselfish. What's happened to you? (LEO *rises, crosses to dining-room doors.*)

BEN. (*Quickly, before* OSCAR *can answer.*) Oscar doesn't mind. (*Crossing* U. L.) Not worth fighting about now, eh, Oscar?

OSCAR. (*Angrily.*) I'll get mine in the end. You can be sure of that. I've got my son's future to think about.

HORACE. (*Sharply.*) Leo? Oh, I see. (*Puts his head back, laughs.* REGINA *looks at him nervously.*) I am beginning to see. Everybody will get theirs.

45

BEN. (*Crossing* R. *to* L. *of* HORACE.) I knew you'd see it. Seventy-five thousand, and that seventy-five thousand will make you a million.

REGINA. (*Steps to table, leaning forward.*) It will, Horace, it will.

HORACE. I believe you. (REGINA *steps back, sits sofa. After a second.*) Now I can understand Oscar's self-sacrifice, but what did you have to promise Marshall Company besides the money you're putting up? (LEO *crosses* D. *to back of settee* L.)

BEN. They wouldn't take promises. They wanted guarantees.

HORACE. Of what?

BEN. (*Nods.*) Water power. Free and plenty of it.

HORACE. You got them that, of course?

BEN. Cheap. You'd think the governor of a great State would make his price a little higher. (*Crossing to chair* L. C.) From pride, you know. (HORACE *smiles.* BEN *smiles.*) Cheap wages. (*Sits chair.*) What do you mean by cheap wages, I say to Marshall? Less than Massachusetts, he says to me, and that averages eight a week. (*Leans back.*) Eight a week! By God, I tell him, *I'd* work for eight a week myself. Why, there ain't a mountain white or a town nigger but wouldn't give his right arm for three silver dollars every week, eh, Horace?

HORACE. Sure. And they'll take less than that when you get around to playing them off against each other. You can save a little money *that* way, Ben. (*Angrily.*) And make them hate each other just a little more than they do now.

REGINA. What's all this about?

BEN. (*Laughs.*) There'll be no trouble from anybody, white or black, Marshall said that to me. "What about strikes? That's all we've had in Massachusetts for the last three years." I say to him, "What's a strike? I never heard of one. Come South, Marshall. We got good folks and we don't stand for any fancy fooling."

HORACE. You're right. (*Slowly.*) Well, it looks like you made a good deal for yourselves, and for Marshall, too. (CAL *has come into dining-room and closes doors. To* BEN.) Your father used to say he made the thousands and you boys would make the millions. I think he was right. (*Rises.*)

REGINA. (*They are all looking at* HORACE. *She laughs, nervously, leans forward.*) Millions for *us*, too.

HORACE. Us? You and me? I don't think so. We've got enough money, Regina. We'll just sit by and watch the boys grow rich.

(*Steps* u. c., *holding on to chair.* OSCAR *sits on piano stool. They watch him tensely, as he begins to move toward staircase. He passes* LEO, *looks at him for a second. Brightly.*) How's everything at the bank, Leo?

LEO. Fine, sir. Everything is fine.

HORACE. How are all the ladies in Mobile? (LEO *draws back.* HORACE *turns, a step to* REGINA, *sharply.*) Whatever made you think I'd let Zan marry ——?

REGINA. (*Crosses above table* R.) Do you mean that you are turning this down? Is it possible that's what you mean?

BEN. (*Nervously, but speaking with good nature—gesturing* RE-GINA *to be quiet.*) No, that's not what he means. Turning down a fortune! Horace is tired. He'd rather talk about it tomorrow ——

REGINA. We can't keep putting it off this way. Oscar must be in Chicago by the end of the week with the money and contracts. (*Crosses to* HORACE.)

OSCAR. (*Giggles, pleased.*) Yes, sir. Got to be there end of the week. (HORACE *crosses* R.) No sense going without the money.

REGINA. (*Tensely.*) I've waited long enough for your answer. I'm not going to wait any longer.

HORACE. (*Crossing to stairs, above* REGINA, *very deliberately.*) I'm very tired now, Regina.

BEN. (*Hastily.*) Now Horace probably has his reasons. Things he'd like explained. Tomorrow will do. I can ——

REGINA. (*Turns to* BEN, *sharply.*) I want to know his reasons now. (*Turns back to* HORACE.)

HORACE. (*As he climbs the steps.*) I don't know them all myself. Let's leave it at that.

REGINA. (*Crosses* U. *to foot of stairs.*) We shall not leave it at that. We have waited for you here like children. Waited for you to come home.

HORACE. So that you could invest my money. So this is why you wanted me home? Well, I had hoped —— (*Quietly.*) If you are disappointed, Regina, I'm sorry. But I must do what I think best. We'll talk about it another day.

REGINA. We'll talk about it now. Just you and me.

HORACE. (*Stops on landing, looks down at her. His voice is tense.*) Please, Regina. It's been a hard trip. I don't feel well. Please leave me alone now.

REGINA. (*Quietly.*) I want to talk to you, Horace. I'm coming up.

(*He looks at her for a moment, then moves on again out of sight. She begins to climb stairs.*)

BEN. (*Softly.* REGINA *turns to him as he speaks.*) Sometimes it is better to wait for the sun to rise again. (*She does not answer.*) And sometimes, as our mother used to tell you, (REGINA *starts upstairs.*) it's unwise for a good-looking woman to frown. (BEN *rises, crosses* U. *to landing.*) Softness and a smile do more to the heart of men —— (*She disappears.* BEN *stands looking up the stairs. A long silence. Then, suddenly,* OSCAR *giggles.*)

OSCAR. Let us hope she'll change his mind. Let us hope. (*After a second* BEN *crosses to table* R., *picks up his newspaper, continues to sofa* R., *sits—begins to read.* OSCAR *looks at* BEN. *The silence makes* LEO *uncomfortable.*)

LEO. (*Steps* R. *to* C.) The paper says twenty-seven cases of Yellow Fever in New Orleans. Guess the flood waters caused it. (*Nobody pays attention.*) Thought they were building levees high enough. Like the niggers always say: a man born of woman can't build nothing high enough for the Mississippi. (*Gets no answer. Gives an embarrassed laugh. Upstairs there is the sound of voices. Voices are not loud, but* BEN, OSCAR, LEO *become conscious of them.* LEO *crosses* U. *to landing, looks up, listens.*)

REGINA. I can't understand what you mean. I can't believe that you mean to turn this down. This is what you've been waiting for, what all of us have been waiting for. You must be going crazy or you must have reasons that you are not telling us.

HORACE. I don't know my reasons. I just don't want it.

REGINA. You don't want it. But I do want it.

OSCAR. (*Pointing up.*) Now just suppose she don't change his mind? Just suppose he keeps on refusing? (LEO *turns back to them, listens.*)

BEN. (*Without conviction.*) He's tired. It was a mistake to talk to him today. He's a sick man but he isn't a crazy one.

OSCAR. (*Giggles.*) But just suppose he is crazy. What then? (LEO *crosses slowly to back of sofa* L.)

BEN. (*Puts down his paper, peers at* OSCAR.) Then we'll go outside for the money. There's plenty who would give it.

OSCAR. And plenty who will want a lot for what they give. The ones who are rich enough to give, will be smart enough to want. That means we'd be working for them, don't it, Ben?

BEN. You don't have to tell me the things I told you six months ago.

OSCAR. Oh, you're right not to worry. She'll change his mind. She always has. (*Silence. Suddenly* REGINA'S *voice becomes louder and sharper. All of them begin to listen now. Slowly* BEN *rises, goes to listen by staircase.* OSCAR, *watching him, smiles. As they listen* REGINA'S *voice becomes very loud.* HORACE'S *voice is no longer heard.*)

REGINA. People don't pass up chances like this. I won't let you pass up chances like this. I won't let you pass up this one just because you've gone crazy!

OSCAR. Maybe.

REGINA. And if you change your mind in a week, it will be too late. It's got to be done now.

HORACE. I won't change my mind. I don't want it.

REGINA. You don't want it but I do want it. I'm your wife. I have a right to expect that you will take care of my future. Of your child's future.

OSCAR. But I don't believe it. I never did believe he was going in with us.

BEN. (*Turning on him—crosses* D. C.) What the hell do you expect me to do?

OSCAR. (*Mildly.*) Nothing. You done your almighty best. Nobody could blame you if the whole thing just dripped away right through our fingers. (BEN *crosses* R. *to sofa for paper.*) You can't do a thing. But there may be something I could do for us. (OSCAR *rises.* BEN *starts to pick up paper but is stopped by* OSCAR'S *words.*) Or, I might better say, (*Crossing to* C.) Leo could do for us. (BEN *stops, turns, looks at* OSCAR. LEO *is staring at* OSCAR. *Turns to* LEO.) Ain't that true, son? (LEO *crosses* D. L.) Ain't it true you might be able to help your own kin-folks?

LEO. (*Nervously taking a step to him.*) Papa, I ——

BEN. (*Slowly.*) How would he help us, Oscar?

OSCAR. Leo's got a friend. (*Crosses to* BEN.) Leo's friend owns eighty-eight thousand dollars in Union Pacific Bonds. (BEN *turns to look at* LEO.) Leo's friend don't look at the bonds much, not for five or six months at a time.

BEN. (*After a pause.*) Union Pacific. Uh, huh. Let me understand. Leo's friend would—would lend him these bonds and he ——?

OSCAR. (*Nods.*) Would be kind enough to lend them to us.

BEN. (*Crossing to* C.) Leo.

LEO. (*Excited, comes to him.*) Yes, sir?

BEN. When would your friend be wanting the bonds back?

LEO. (*Very nervous.*) I don't know. I—well, I ——

OSCAR. (*Sharply—step to him.*) You told me he won't look at them until fall ——

LEO. Oh. That's right. But I —— Not till fall. Uncle Horace never ——

BEN. (*Sharply.*) Be still.

OSCAR. (*Smiles at* LEO—*crosses to* C.) Your uncle doesn't wish to know your friend's name.

LEO. (*Starts to laugh.*) That's a good one. Not know his name ——

OSCAR. Shut up, Leo! (LEO *turns away slowly, moves to table* L. BEN *turns to* OSCAR.) He won't look at them again until September. That gives us five months. Leo will return the bonds in three months. And we'll have no trouble raising the money once the mills are going up. Will Marshall accept bonds? (BEN *stops to listen to sudden sharp voices from above. The voices are now very angry and very loud.*)

REGINA. I have a right to expect that.

HORACE. Please go away and leave me alone.

REGINA. I won't leave you alone. I demand that you put up this money and I demand that you do it immediately.

BEN. (*Then smiling.*) Why not? Why not? (*Laughs—to* OSCAR.) Good. We are lucky. We'll take the loan from Leo's friend—I think he will make a safer partner than our sister. (*Nods toward stairs. Turns to* LEO.) How soon can you get them?

LEO. Today. Right now. (*Step to* BEN.) They're in the safe deposit box and ——

BEN. (*Sharply.*) I don't want to know where they are.

OSCAR. (*Laughs.*) We will keep it secret from you. (*Pats* BEN'S *arm.*)

BEN. (*Smiles.*) Good. Draw a check for our part. You can take the night train for Chicago. (*To* OSCAR.) Well, Oscar, (*Holds out his hand—*OSCAR *takes it, they shake hands.*) good luck to us. (*Crosses* R. *to table.*)

OSCAR. (*Turns to* BEN.) Leo will be taken care of?

LEO. I'm entitled to Uncle Horace's share. I'd enjoy being a partner ——

BEN. (*Turns to stare at him.*) You would? You can go to hell, you little —— (*Starts toward* LEO.)

OSCAR. (*Nervously, stopping* BEN.) Now, now. He didn't mean that. I only want to be sure he'll get something out of all this.

BEN. Of course. We'll take care of him. We won't have any trouble about that. I'll see you at the store.

OSCAR. (*Nods.*) That's settled then. Come on, son. (*Starts for door.*)

LEO. (*Puts out his hand—crosses to* BEN.) I didn't mean just that. I was only going to say what a great day this was for me and —— (BEN *ignores his hand.*)

BEN. Go on. (*Crosses* R. *to front of table.* LEO *looks at him, turns, follows* OSCAR *out.* BEN *stands where he is, thinking. Again voices upstairs can be heard.* REGINA'S *is high and furious.* BEN *looks up, smiles, winces at the noise.*)

REGINA. Nobody would turn this down. You must have your reasons. You must have reasons you won't talk about. (*The noise of fists pounding against a door is heard, and* ALEXANDRA'S *voice.*)

ALEXANDRA. Mama—Mama—don't —— (*Noise of running footsteps is heard, and* ALEXANDRA *comes running down the steps, speaking as she comes, together with voices upstairs.*)

REGINA. What are they? What possible reasons could there be? I demand to know. All my life I've had to force you to make something out of yourself.

HORACE. Let me alone.

REGINA. I won't let you alone. If I'd let you alone you'd still be working for somebody else.

HORACE. So that's why you wanted me home?

REGINA. Yes, that's the reason.

HORACE. Then it's a bad one. Because it won't work.

REGINA. Did you think I wanted you home for yourself? Is that what you thought?

ALEXANDRA. (*Almost crying. On landing.*) Uncle Ben! (*Coming downstairs.*) Uncle Ben! (BEN *crosses* U. C.) Please go up. Please make Mama stop. Uncle Ben, he's sick, he's so sick. How can Mama talk to him like that—please, make her stop. She'll——

BEN. Alexandra, you have a tender heart.

ALEXANDRA. Go on up, Uncle Ben, please —— (*Suddenly noise from above stops, and a second later there is the sound of a door opening and then being slammed.*)

BEN. Now you see. Everything is over. Don't worry. (*He starts for door.* ALEXANDRA *crosses* D. *to above chair* L. C.) Alexandra, I want you to tell your mother how sorry I am that I had to leave. (*Crosses to hall.*) And don't worry so, my dear. Married folk frequently raise their voices, unfortunately. (*He starts to put on his hat and coat as* REGINA *appears on stairs. When she speaks to* BEN, *her voice is cold and calm.*)

ALEXANDRA. (*Furiously—turns, crosses* U. *to landing.*) How can you treat Papa like this! He's sick. He's very sick. Don't you know that! I won't let you.

REGINA. Mind your business, Alexandra. (ALEXANDRA *turns down to above settee* L., *facing* L. *To* BEN *on landing.*) How much longer can you wait for the money?

BEN. (*Putting on his coat—steps in.*) He has refused? My, that's too bad.

REGINA. He will change his mind. I'll find a way to make him. What's the longest you can wait now?

BEN. I could wait until next week. (*Steps in.*) But I can't wait until next week. (*He giggles, pleased at the joke.*) I could but I can't. Could and can't. Well, I must go now. I'm very late —— (*He starts.*)

REGINA. (*Coming downstairs toward him.*) You're not going. I want to talk to you. (*She crosses into room.*)

BEN. (*Looks at her, crosses* D. *to her.*) Oh, I was about to give Alexandra a message for you. I wanted to tell you that Oscar is going to Chicago tonight, so we can't be here for our usual Friday supper.

REGINA. (*Tensely.*) Oscar is going to Chi —— (*Softly.*) What do you mean?

BEN. Just that. Everything is settled. He's going on to deliver to Marshall ——

REGINA. (*Taking a step to him.*) I demand to know what —— You are lying. You are trying to scare me. *You haven't got the money.* How could you have it? You can't have—(BEN *laughs.*) you will wait until I —— (HORACE *comes into view on landing.*)

BEN. You are getting out of hand. Since when do I take orders from you? (*He turns.*)

REGINA. Wait, you —— (BEN *stops.* REGINA *steps to him.*) How can he go to Chicago? Did a ghost arrive with the money? (BEN *starts for hall.*) I don't believe you. Come back here. (REGINA *starts after him.*) Come back here, you—— (*The door slams. She stops in the doorway, staring, her fists clenched. After a pause she turns slowly and steps into the room.*)

HORACE. (*Standing on landing of the stairs, very quietly.*) It's a great day when you and Ben cross swords. I've been waiting for it for years.

ALEXANDRA. Papa, Papa, (*Crosses* U. *to below landing.*) please go back! You will——

HORACE. And so they don't need you, and so you will not have your millions, after all?

REGINA. (*Turns slowly.*) You hate to see anybody live now, don't you? You hate to think that I'm going to be alive and have what I want. (*Comes toward stairs, looking up at him.*)

HORACE. I should have known you'd think that was the reason.

REGINA. Because you're going to die and you know you're going to die.

ALEXANDRA. (*Shrilly.*) Mama! Don't—don't listen, Papa. Just don't listen. Go away——

HORACE. Not to keep you from getting what you want. Not even partly that. (*Steps down one step, holding on to rail, leaning over to look down at her.*) I'm sick of you, sick of this house, sick of my life here. I'm sick of your brothers and their dirty tricks to make a dime. (ALEXANDRA *turns away, crosses* D. *to back of settee.*) There must be better ways of getting rich than cheating niggers on a pound of bacon. Why should I give you the money? (*Very angrily.*) To pound the bones of this town to make dividends for you to spend? You wreck the town, you and your brothers, *you* wreck the town and live on it. Not me. Maybe it's easy for the dying to be honest. But it's not my fault I'm dying. (ADDIE *enters* L., *stands at door quietly.*) I'll do no more harm now. I've done enough. I'll die my own way. And I'll do it without making the world any worse. I leave that to you.

REGINA. (*Looks up at him slowly, calmly.*) I hope you die. I hope you die soon. (*Smiles.*) I'll be waiting for you to die.

ALEXANDRA. (*Shrieking.*) Papa! Don't—don't listen—don't——

ADDIE. Come here, Zan. Come out of this room. (ALEXANDRA *runs quickly to* ADDIE, *who holds her in her arms.* HORACE *turns slowly and starts upstairs.*)

MEDIUM CURTAIN

ACT III

SCENE: *Same as Act J. Jwo weeks later. Jt is late after-noon and it is raining.*

AT RISE: HORACE *is sitting near the window in a wheel chair. On the table next to him is a safe deposit box, and one small bottle of medicine and spoon.* BIRDIE *and* ALEXANDRA *are playing the piano. On the chair* R. *of table* U. C. *is a large sewing basket.*

A phrase of the song is played before the curtain rises. As the curtain is going up the song is reaching its con-clusion.

BIRDIE. (*Counting for* ALEXANDRA.) One and two and three and four. One and two and three and four. (*They finish song and laugh.* ALEXANDRA *repeats a phrase. Nods—turns to* HORACE.) We used to play together, Horace. Remember?

HORACE. (*Has been looking out of window.*) What, Birdie?

BIRDIE. We played together. You and me.

ALEXANDRA. (*Stops playing, looks to* HORACE, *then* BIRDIE.) Papa used to play?

BIRDIE. Indeed he did. (ADDIE *appears at door* L. *in a large kitchen apron. She is wiping her hands on a towel.*) He played the fiddle and very well, too. (*Jurns to piano and starts playing.*)

ALEXANDRA. (*Jurns to smile at* HORACE.) I never knew ——

ADDIE. Where's your Mama?

ALEXANDRA. Gone to Miss Safronia's to fit her dresses. (ADDIE *nods, starts to exit.*)

HORACE. Addie.

ADDIE. (*Crossing to* C.) Yes, Mr. Horace.

HORACE. (*Speaks as if he had made a sudden decision.*) Tell Cal to get on his things. I want him to go an errand. (ADDIE *nods, exits* L. HORACE *moves nervously in his chair, looks out of window.*)

ALEXANDRA. (*Who has been watching him.*) It's too bad it's been

54

raining all day, Papa. But you can go out in the yard tomorrow. Don't be restless.

HORACE. I'm not restless, darling. (ALEXANDRA *turns to piano and joins* BIRDIE *in playing, after playing one measure together* BIRDIE *stops and turns to* HORACE. ALEXANDRA *continues playing alone.*)

BIRDIE. I remember so well the time we played together, (*To* ALEXANDRA.) your Papa and me. (*To* HORACE.) It was the first time Oscar brought me here to supper. I had never seen all the Hubbards together before, (*To* ALEXANDRA.) and you know what a ninny I am and how shy. (*Turns to look at* HORACE.) You said you could play the fiddle, (*Rises, crosses to table* U. C.) and you'd be much obliged if I'd play with you. (*Pouring glass of water.*) I was obliged to you, all right, all right. (*Laughs when he does not answer her.*) Horace, (*Steps to him, holding glass.*) you haven't heard a word I've said.

HORACE. Birdie, when did Oscar get back from Chicago?

BIRDIE. Yesterday. Hasn't he been here yet?

ALEXANDRA. (*Stops playing.*) No. Neither has Uncle Ben since— since that day.

BIRDIE. Oh, (*To* ALEXANDRA.) I didn't know it was *that* bad. (*Turns to* HORACE.) Oscar never tells me anything ——

HORACE. (*Smiles, nods.*) The Hubbards have had their great quarrel. I knew it would come some day. (*Laughs.*) It came.

ALEXANDRA. It came. It certainly came all right.

BIRDIE. (*Amazed.*) But Oscar was in such a good humor when he got home, (ADDIE *enters.*) I didn't ——

HORACE. Yes, I can understand that. (ADDIE *is carrying large tray with three water glasses, a carafe of elderberry wine and a plate of cookies, which she puts on table* D. L. BIRDIE *hurries to* ADDIE, *leaving water glass on table* U. C.)

ALEXANDRA. Addie! A party! What for?

ADDIE. (*Pouring wine into the three glasses.*) Nothing for. I had the fresh butter so I made the cakes, and a little elderberry does the stomach good in the rain. (ADDIE *looks at* HORACE, *then crosses to* C., *moves chair* R. C. *upstage, then crosses to him, moves him to* C., L. *of table* R.)

BIRDIE. (*Takes her glass and puts* ALEXANDRA'S *on piano.*) Isn't this nice! A party just for us. Let's play party music, Zan. (ALEXANDRA *begins to play a gay piece.*)

ADDIE. (*To* HORACE, *wheeling his chair to* C.) Come over here,

Mr. Horace, and don't be thinking so much. (*She crosses to table* L. *for* HORACE'S *glass, brings it to him.* ALEXANDRA *stops playing, turns and watches him.*) A glass of elderberry will do more good. (ALEXANDRA *reaches for another cake,* BIRDIE *pours herself another glass of wine.*)

ALEXANDRA. (*Her mouth full.*) Good cakes, Addie. It's nice here. Just us. Be nice if it could always be this way.

BIRDIE. (*Nods, happily.*) Quiet and restful. (*Drinks, then crosses to piano stool, sits.*)

ADDIE. (*Crossing to table* U. C., *lights lamp.*) Well, it won't be that way long. Little while now, even sitting here, you'll hear the red bricks going into place. The next day the smoke'll be pushing out the chimneys (ALEXANDRA *crosses to chair at piano, sits.*) and by church time that Sunday every human born of woman will be living on chicken. (*Crossing* R. *to mantel.*) That's how Mr. Ben's been telling the story.

HORACE. (*Looks at her.*) They believe it that way?

ADDIE. Believe it? (*Placing footstool so that she can reach upstage lamp on mantel.* BIRDIE *crosses to table, pours another drink.*) They use to believing what Mr. Ben orders. There ain't been so much talk around here since Sherman's army didn't come near. (*Lights upper mantel lamp.*)

HORACE. (*Softly.*) They are fools.

ADDIE. (*Nods.*) You ain't born in the South unless you're a fool. (ADDIE *moves footstool to downstage end of mantel, and lights lower mantel lamp.*)

BIRDIE. (*Has drunk another glass. She has been listening to the others.*) But we didn't play together after that night. (*Crosses to front settee* L.) Oscar said he didn't like me to play on the piano. (*Turns to* ALEXANDRA.) You know what he said that night? (ADDIE *crosses to chair* U. C., *gets sewing basket, crosses to chair* D. R., *turns it to face them, sits.*)

ALEXANDRA. Who?

BIRDIE. Oscar. He said that music made him nervous. He said he just sat and waited for the next note. (ALEXANDRA *laughs.*) He wasn't poking fun. He meant it. Ah, well —— (*She finishes her glass, shakes her head.* HORACE *looks at her, smiles. Crossing to* HORACE.) Your Papa don't like to admit it, but he's been mighty kind to me all these years. (*Running the back of her hand along his sleeve.*) Often he'd step in when somebody said something and

once —— (*She stops, turns away, her face still.*) Once he stopped
Oscar from —— (*She stops, turns, steps* U. S. *Quickly.*) I'm sorry
I said that. (*Crossing* L. *back of settee.*) Why, here I am so happy
and yet I think about bad things. (*Laughs nervously.*) That's not
right, now is it? (*Crosses to table* L., *pours drink, crosses to upper
end piano.* CAL *appears in the door* L. *He has on an old coat and
is carrying a torn umbrella.*)

ALEXANDRA. Have a cake, Cal.

CAL. (*Comes in, takes a cake.*) Yes'm. You want me, Mr. Horace?
(*Crosses* C. *to* L. *of* HORACE.)

HORACE. What time is it, Cal? (*Puts glass on table.*)

CAL. 'Bout ten minutes before it's five.

HORACE. All right. Now you walk yourself down to the bank.
(ALEXANDRA *starts to play softly.*)

CAL. It'll be closed. Nobody'll be there but Mr. Mander, Mr. Joe
Horns, Mr. Leo ——

HORACE. Go in the back way. They'll be at the table, going over
the day's business. (*Points to deposit box.*) See that box?

CAL. (*Nods.*) Yes, sir.

HORACE. You tell Mander that Mr. Horace says he's much obliged
to him for bringing the box, it arrived all right.

CAL. (*Bewildered.*) He know you got the box. He bring it hisself
Wednesday. I opened the door to him and he say, " Hello, Cal,
coming on to summer weather ——"

HORACE. You say just what I tell you. Understand? (BIRDIE
crosses to table L., *pours drink, stands at table.*)

CAL. No, sir. I ain't going to say I understand. I'm going down
and tell a man he give you something he already know he give
you, and you say " understand."

HORACE. Now, Cal ——

CAL. Yes, sir. I just going to say you obliged for the box coming
all right. I ain't going to understand it, but I'm going to say
it ——

HORACE. And tell him I want him to come over here after supper,
and to bring Mr. Sol Fowler with him. (ALEXANDRA *playing.*)

CAL. (*Nods.*) He's to come after supper and bring Mr. Sol Fowler,
your attorney-at-law, with him.

HORACE. (*Smiles.*) That's right. Just walk right in the back room
and say your piece. (*Slowly.*) In front of everybody.

57

CAL. (*Takes step to* HORACE, *then turns away* L.) Yes, sir. (*Mumbles to himself as he exits* L.)

ALEXANDRA. (*Who has been watching* HORACE.) Is anything the matter, Papa?

HORACE. Oh, no. Nothing.

ADDIE. (*Watching* BIRDIE *take another glass of wine.*) Miss Birdie, that elderberry going to give you a headache spell.

BIRDIE. (*Beginning to be drunk. Gaily.*) Oh, I don't think so. I don't think it will. (*Drinks.*)

ALEXANDRA. (*As* HORACE *puts his hand to his throat. Rises, crosses to his* L.) Do you want your medicine, Papa?

HORACE. No, no. I'm all right, darling.

BIRDIE. (*At* L. *of table* L.) Mama used to give me elderberry wine when I was a little girl. For hiccoughs. (*Laughs.*) You know, I don't think people get hiccoughs any more. Isn't that funny? (BIRDIE *laughs.* HORACE *and* ALEXANDRA *laugh, too.*) I used to get hiccoughs just when I shouldn't have. (*Crosses to piano, sits, starts playing, drinks.*)

ADDIE. (*Nods.*) And nobody get growing pains no more. That is funny. Just as if there was some style in what you get. One year an ailment's stylish (BIRDIE *stops playing.*) and the next year, it ain't.

BIRDIE. (*Turns to them.*) I remember. It was my first big party, at Lionnet I mean, and I was so excited, (*Rises, crosses to table* L.) and there I was with hiccoughs and Mama laughing. (*Softly. Looking at carafe.*) Mama always laughed. (*Picks up carafe.*) A big party, a lovely dress from Mr. Worth in Paris, France, and hiccoughs. (*Pours drink.*) My brother pounding me on the back and Mama with the elderberry bottle, laughing at me. Everybody was on their way to come, and I was such a ninny, hiccoughing away. (*Drinks. Pauses.*) You know, that was the first day I ever saw Oscar Hubbard. (*Crosses to* C.) The Ballongs were selling their hosses and he was going there to buy. He passed and lifted his hat—we could see him from the window—and my brother, to tease Mama, said maybe we should have invited the Hubbards to the party. He said Mama didn't like them because they kept a store, and he said that was old-fashioned of her. (*Her face lights up—looking out.*) And then, and then, I saw Mama angry for the first time in my life. She said that wasn't the reason. She said she was old-fashioned, but not that way. She said she was old-fash-

58

ioned enough not to like people who killed animals they couldn't use, and who made their money charging awful interest to poor, ignorant niggers and cheating them on what they bought. She was very angry, Mama was. I had never seen her face like that. And then suddenly she laughed and said, " Look, I've frightened Birdie out of the hiccoughs." (*Her head drops, then softly.*) And so she had. They were all gone. (*Moves up to sofa* L., *sits.* ALEXANDRA *crosses* L. *to chair* L. C.)

ADDIE. (*To her sewing.*) Yeah, they got mighty well off cheating niggers. (*To them.*) Well, there are people who eat the earth and eat all the people on it like in the Bible with the locusts. Then, there are people who stand around and watch them eat it. (*Softly.*) Sometimes I think it ain't right to stand and watch them do it.

BIRDIE. (*Thoughtfully.*) Like I say, if we could only go back to Lionnet. Everybody'd be better there. They'd be good and kind. I like people to be kind. (*Pours drink.*) Don't you, Horace, don't you like people to be kind?

HORACE. Yes, Birdie.

BIRDIE. (*Very drunk now.*) Yes, that was the first day I ever saw Oscar. Who would have thought ——? (*Drink. Quickly—caressing the glass.*) You all want to know something? Well, I don't like Leo. My very own son, and I don't like him. (*Laughs, gaily.*) My, I guess, I even like Oscar more. (*Drinks.*)

ALEXANDRA. (*A step to* BIRDIE.) Why did you marry Uncle Oscar?

ADDIE. (*Sharply.*) That's no question for you to be asking.

HORACE. (*Sharply.*) Why not? She's heard enough around here to ask anything.

ALEXANDRA. Aunt Birdie, why did you marry Uncle Oscar?

BIRDIE. (*Places glass on table. Pleasantly.*) I don't know. I thought I liked him. He was so kind to me and I thought it was because he liked me, too. But that wasn't the reason —— (*Wheels on* ALEXANDRA.) Ask why *he* married *me!* I can tell you that: he's told it to me often enough.

ADDIE. (*Leaning forward.*) Miss Birdie, don't ——

BIRDIE. (*Speaking very rapidly, tensely.*) My family was good and the cotton on Lionnet's fields was better. Ben Hubbard wanted the cotton and (*Rises.*) Oscar Hubbard married it for him. (ALEXANDRA *crosses to* HORACE.) He was kind to me, then. He used to smile at me. He hasn't smiled at me since. Everybody knew that's what he married me for. (ADDIE *rises.*) Everybody but me. (*Turns *away, crosses* D. L.) Stupid, stupid me. (ADDIE *puts sewing basket on chair, takes step to* HORACE.)

ALEXANDRA. (*To* HORACE, *holding his hand, softly.*) I see. (*Hesitates.*) Papa, I mean—when you feel better couldn't we go away? I mean, by ourselves. Couldn't we find a way to go ——

HORACE. (*Placing his hand over hers.*) Yes, I know what you mean. We'll try to find a way. I promise you, darling.

ADDIE. (*Looks at them for a second, then goes* L. *to* BIRDIE.) Rest a bit, Miss Birdie. You get talking like this you'll get a headache and ——

BIRDIE. (*Sharply turning to her.*) I've never had a headache in my life. (*Crosses* U. L. *Begins to cry, hysterically.*) You know it as well as I do. (*Turns to* ALEXANDRA. *Crossing to her back of settee.* ADDIE *crosses* U. L.) I never had a headache, Zan. That's a lie they tell for me. *I drink.* All by myself, in my own room, by myself, *I drink.* Then, when they want to hide it, they say, " Birdie's got a headache again ——"

ALEXANDRA. (*Comes to her, quickly.*) Aunt Birdie. (ADDIE *turns to look at them.*)

BIRDIE. (*Turning away.*) Even you won't like me now. You won't like me, any more.

ALEXANDRA. I love you. I'll always love you.

BIRDIE. (*Furiously.*) Well, don't. (*Turns to* ALEXANDRA.) Don't love me. Because in twenty years you'll just be like me. They'll do all the same things to you. (*Begins to laugh, hysterically.*) You know what? In twenty-two years I haven't had a whole day of happiness. Oh, a little, like today with you all. But never a single, whole day. I say to myself, if only I had one more *whole* day, then —— (*The laugh stops.*) And that's the way you'll be. And you'll trail after them, just like me, hoping they won't be so mean that day or say something to make you feel so bad—only you'll be worse off because you haven't got my Mama to remember —— (*Turns away, her head drops. She stands quietly, swaying a little, holding onto sofa.* ALEXANDRA *leans down, puts her cheek on* BIRDIE'S *arm.*)

ALEXANDRA. (*To* BIRDIE.) I guess we were all trying to make a happy day. You know, we sit around and try to pretend nothing's happened. We try to pretend we are not here. We make believe we are just by ourselves, some place else, and it doesn't seem to work. (*Kisses* BIRDIE'S *hand, which she has been holding.*) Come now, Aunt Birdie, I'll walk you home. You and me. (*She takes* BIRDIE'S *arm, they move slowly out. In the hallway* ALEXANDRA *places a raincoat over* BIRDIE'S *shoulders. They exit.* ADDIE *and* HORACE *are silent.*)

ADDIE. Well. (*Sighs.*) First time I ever heard Miss Birdie say a word. (*Crossing* R. *to table* R. HORACE *looks at her.*) Maybe it's good for her. (*Picks up glass from table* R.) I'm just sorry Zan had to hear it. (*Takes glass to table* U. C. HORACE *moves his head as if he were uncomfortable.*) You feel bad, don't you? (*He shrugs.*)

HORACE. So you didn't want Zan to hear? It would be nice to let her stay innocent, like Birdie at her age. Let her listen now. Let her see everything. How else is she going to know that she's got to get away? I'm trying to show her that. I'm trying, but I've only got a little time left. She can even hate me when I'm dead, if she'll only learn to hate and fear this.

ADDIE. Mr. Horace ——

HORACE. Pretty soon there'll be nobody to help her but you.

ADDIE. (*Crossing to him.*) What can I do?

HORACE. Take her away.

ADDIE. How can I do that? Do you think they'd let me just go away with her ——?

HORACE. I'll fix it so they can't stop you when you're ready to go. You'll go, Addie?

ADDIE. (*After a second, softly.*) Yes, sir, I promise. (*He touches her arm, nods.*)

HORACE. (*After a second, quietly.*) I'm going to have Sol Fowler make me a new will. They'll make trouble, but you make Zan stand firm and Fowler'll do the rest. (*She looks at him, nods, crosses* R., *front table.*) Addie, (*She turns to* HORACE.) I'd like to leave you something for yourself. I always wanted to.

ADDIE. (*Laughs.*) Don't you do that, Mr. Horace. A nigger woman in a white man's will! I'd never get it nohow.

HORACE. I know. But upstairs in the armoire drawer there's seventeen hundred-dollar bills. It's money left from my trip. It's in an envelope with your name. It's for you.

ADDIE. Seventeen hundred-dollar bills! My God, Mr. Horace, I won't know how to count up that high. (*Shyly.*) It's mighty kind and good of you. I don't know what to say for thanks ——

CAL. (*Appears in doorway.*) I'm back. (*Stands umbrella in* U. L. *corner. No answer. Crossing to* C.) I'm back.

ADDIE. (*Crossing* R. *to chair* D. R., *picks up basket, sits.*) So we see.

HORACE. Well?

CAL. Nothing. I just went down and spoke my piece. Just like you told me, I say Mr. Horace he thank you mightily for the safe box arriving in good shape and he say you come right after supper to his house and bring Mr. Attorney-at-Law Sol Fowler with you. Then I wipe my hands on my coat. Every time I ever told a lie in my whole life, I wipe my hands right after. Can't help doing it. Well, while I'm wiping my hands, Mr. Leo jump up and say to me, "What box! What you talking about?"

HORACE. (*Smiles.*) Did he?

CAL. And Mr. Leo say he got to leave a little early 'cause he got something to do. And then Mr. Mander say Mr. Leo should sit right down and finish up his work and stop acting like somebody made him Mr. President. So he sit down. Now, just like I told you, Mr. Mander was mighty surprised with the message because he knows right well he brought the box —— (*Pointing to box. Sighs.*) But he took it all right. Some men take everything easy and some do not.

HORACE. (*Puts his head back, laughs.*) Mr. Leo was telling the truth: he *has* got something to do. I hope Mander don't keep him too long. (*Outside there is the sound of voices.* CAL *exits* R. ADDIE *crosses quickly to* HORACE, *puts basket on table* R., *begins to wheel his chair toward the stairs. Sharply.*) No. Leave me where I am.

ADDIE. (*Step* D. *to his* L.) But that's Miss Regina coming back.

HORACE. (*Nods, looking at door.*) Go away, Addie.

ADDIE. (*Hesitates.*) Mr. Horace. Don't talk no more today. You don't feel well and it won't do no good ——

HORACE. (*As he hears footsteps in hall.*) Go on. (*She looks at him for a second, then picks up her sewing from table* R. *and exits* L. *as* REGINA *comes in from hall.* HORACE'S *chair is now so placed that he is in front of table with the medicine.* REGINA *stands in the hall, shakes umbrella, stands it in* U. R. *corner, takes off her cloak and throws it over bannister. She stares at* HORACE.)

REGINA. (*As she takes off her gloves, crossing to* C.) We had agreed that you were to stay in your part of this house and I in mine. This room is my part of the house. Please don't come down here again.

62

HORACE. I won't.

REGINA. (*Crosses* D. R. *toward bell-cord below mantel.*) I'll get Cal to take you upstairs.

HORACE. (*Smiles.*) Before you do I want to tell you that after all, we have invested our money in Hubbard, Sons and Marshall, Cotton Manufacturers.

REGINA. (*Stops, turns, stares at him.*) What are you talking about? You haven't seen Ben —— When did you change your mind?

HORACE. I didn't change my mind. I didn't invest the money. (*Smiles at the expression on her face.*) It was invested for me.

REGINA. (*Angrily.*) What ——?

HORACE. I had eighty-eight thousand dollars' worth of Union Pacific bonds in that safe deposit box. They are not there now. Go and look. (*As she stares at him. Points to box.*) Go and look, Regina. (*She crosses quickly to box, opens it. He speaks when she is at table.*) Those bonds are as negotiable as money. (*She closes box.*)

REGINA. (*Turns back to him.*) What kind of joke are you playing now? Is this for my benefit?

HORACE. I don't look in that box very often, but three days ago, on Wednesday it was, because I had made a decision ——

REGINA. I want to know what you are talking about.

HORACE. (*Sharply.*) Don't interrupt me again. (REGINA *stiffens.*) Because I had made a decision, I sent for the box. The bonds were gone. Eighty-eight thousand dollars gone. (*He smiles at her.*)

REGINA. (*After a moment's silence, quietly crossing* U. C.) Do you think I'm crazy enough to believe what you're saying?

HORACE. (*Shrugs.*) Believe anything you like.

REGINA. (*Stares at him, slowly.*) Where did they go to?

HORACE. They are in Chicago. With Mr. Marshall, I should guess.

REGINA. (*Crossing* D. *to chair* L. C.) What did they do? Walk to Chicago? Have you really gone crazy?

HORACE. Leo took the bonds.

REGINA. (*Turns sharply then speaks softly, without conviction.*) I don't believe it.

HORACE. (*Leans forward.*) I wasn't there but I can guess what happened. (REGINA *sits chair* L. C.) This fine gentleman, to whom you were willing to marry your daughter, took the keys and opened the box. You remember that the day of the fight, Oscar went to Chicago? Well, he went with my bonds that his son Leo

63

had stolen for him. (*Pleasantly.*) And for Ben, of course, too.

REGINA. (*Slowly, nods.*) When did you find out the bonds were gone?

HORACE. Wednesday night.

REGINA. I thought that's what you said. Why have you waited three days to do anything? (*Suddenly laughs.*) This *will* make a fine story.

HORACE. (*Nods.*) Couldn't it?

REGINA. (*Still laughing. Rises, crosses* U. L.—*takes off hat.*) A fine story to hold over their heads. How could they be such fools? (*Turns to him back of settee.*)

HORACE. But I'm not going to hold it over their heads.

REGINA. (*The laugh stops.*) What?

HORACE. (*Turns his chair to face* L.) I'm going to let them keep the bonds—as a loan from you. An eighty-eight thousand dollar loan; they should be grateful to you. They will be, I think.

REGINA. (*Slowly, smiles.*) I see. You are punishing me. But I won't let you punish me. If you won't do anything, I will. Now. (*She starts for door.*)

HORACE. You won't do anything. Because you can't. (REGINA *stops above chair* R. C.) It won't do you any good to make trouble because I shall simply say that I lent them the bonds.

REGINA. (*Slowly.*) You would do that?

HORACE. Yes. (REGINA *crosses* D. *to chair* L. C.) For once in your life I am tying your hands. There is nothing for you to do. (*There is silence. Then she sits down.*)

REGINA. I see. You are going to lend them the bonds and let them keep all the profit they make on them, and there is nothing I can do about it. Is that right?

HORACE. Yes.

REGINA. (*Softly.*) Why did you say that I was making this gift?

HORACE. I was coming to that. I am going to make a new will, Regina, leaving you eighty-eight thousand dollars in Union Pacific bonds. The rest will go to Zan. It's true that your brothers have borrowed your share for a little while. After my death I advise you to talk to Ben and Oscar. They won't admit anything and Ben, I think, will be smart enough to see that he's *safe.* Because I knew about the theft and said nothing. Nor *will* I say anything as long as I live. Is that clear to you?

REGINA. (*Nods, softly, without looking at him.*) You will not say anything as long as you live.

HORACE. That's right. And by that time they will probably have replaced your bonds, and then they'll belong to you and nobody but us will ever know what happened. (*Stops, smiles.*) They'll be around any minute to see what I am going to do. I took good care to see that word reached Leo. They'll be mighty relieved to know I'm going to do nothing and Ben will think it all a capital joke on you. And that will be the end of that. There's nothing you can do to them, nothing you can do to me.

REGINA. You hate me very much.

HORACE. No.

REGINA. Oh, I think you do. (*Puts her head back, sighs.*) Well, we haven't been very good together. Anyway, I don't hate you either. I have only contempt for·you. I've always had.

HORACE. From the very first?

REGINA. I think so.

HORACE. I was in love with *you*. But why did *you* marry *me*?

REGINA. I was lonely when I was young.

HORACE. *You* were lonely?

REGINA. Not the way people usually mean. Lonely for all the things I wasn't going to get. Everything in this house was so busy and there was so little place for what I wanted. I wanted the world. Then, and then—(*Smiles.*) Papa died and left the money to Ben and Oscar.

HORACE. And you married me?

REGINA. Yes, I thought—but I was wrong. You were a small-town clerk then. You haven't changed.

HORACE. (*Nods, smiles.*) And that wasn't what you wanted.

REGINA. No. No, it wasn't what I wanted. (*Pauses, leans back, pleasantly.*) It took me a little while to find out I had made a mistake. As for you—I don't know. It was almost as if I couldn't stand the kind of man you were —— (*Smiles, softly.*) I used to lie there at night, praying you wouldn't come near ——

HORACE. Really? It was as bad as that?

REGINA. (*Nods.*) Remember when I went to Doctor Sloan and I told you he said there was something the matter with me and that you shouldn't touch me any more?

HORACE. I remember.

REGINA. But you believed it? I couldn't understand that. I couldn't understand that anybody could be such a soft fool. That was when I began to despise you.

HORACE. (*Puts his hand to his throat, glances around at bottle of medicine on table, then to her.*) Why didn't you leave me?

REGINA. I told you I married you for something. It turned out it was only for this. (*Carefully.*) This wasn't what I wanted, but it was something. I never thought about it much, but if I had, (HORACE *puts his hand to his throat.*) I'd have known that you would die before I would. But I couldn't have known that you would get heart trouble so early and so bad. I'm lucky, Horace. I've always been lucky. (HORACE *turns slowly to medicine.*) I'll be lucky again. (HORACE *looks at her. Then he puts his hand to his throat. Because he cannot reach the bottle he moves the chair closer. He reaches for medicine, takes out cork, picks up spoon, tries to pour some in the spoon, the bottle slips out of his shaking fingers, and crashes on the table. He draws in his breath, gasps.*)

HORACE. Please. Tell Addie—the other bottle is upstairs. (*She has not moved. She does not move now. He stares at her. Then, suddenly as if he understood, he raises his voice. It is a panic-stricken whisper, too small to be heard outside the room.*) Addie! Addie! Come —— (*Stops as he hears the softness of his voice. He makes a sudden, furious spring from the chair to the stairs, taking the first few steps as if he were a desperate runner. On the fourth step he slips, gasps, grasps the rail, makes a great effort to reach the landing. When he reaches the landing, he is on his knees. His knees give way, he falls on the landing, out of view.* REGINA *has not turned during his climb up the stairs. Now she waits a second. Then she goes below the landing, speaks up.*)

REGINA. Horace. (*When there is no answer, she turns, crosses to door* L., *opens door, calls.*) Addie! Cal! Come in here. (*Crosses* R. *Starts up the steps. When she is on first step,* ADDIE *appears, followed by* CAL. *Both run toward stairs.*) He's had an attack. Come up here. (*They run up steps quickly, passing* REGINA.)

CAL. My God! Mr. Horace ——

REGINA. (*They cannot be seen now. Her voice comes from the head of the stairs.*) Be still, Cal. Bring him in here. (*Before footsteps and voices have completely died away,* ALEXANDRA *appears in hall door, in her raincloak and hood. She comes into room, begins to unfasten cloak, suddenly looks around, sees empty wheel chair, stares, begins to move swiftly as if to look in dining-room.*

At the same moment, ADDIE *runs downstairs. She turns and stares up at* ADDIE.)

ALEXANDRA. Addie! What?

ADDIE. (*Takes* ALEXANDRA *by the shoulders.*) I'm going for the doctor. Go upstairs. (ALEXANDRA *looks at her, then quickly breaks away and runs up the steps.* ADDIE *exits* L. *The stage is empty for a minute. Then the front doorbell begins to ring. When there is no answer it rings again. A second later* LEO *appears in the hall, talking as he comes in.*)

LEO. (*Very nervous.*) Hello. (*Irritably.*) Never saw any use ringing a bell when a door was open. If you are going to ring a bell, then somebody should answer it. (*Gets in the room, looks around, puzzled, listens, hears no sound.*) Aunt Regina. (*Puts hat on sofa* R. *No answer. He moves around restlessly, crossing* L.) Addie. (*Waits, turns, crossing* C.) Where the hell ——? (*Crosses* D. R. *to bell cord, rings it impatiently, twice, waits and gets no answer,* calls.) Cal! (*Rings again, then calls.*) Cal —— (*After a second* CAL *appears on stair landing.*)

CAL. (*His voice is soft, shaken.*) Mr. Leo, Miss Regina says you stop that screaming noise.

LEO. (*Angrily crosses to table* R.) Where is everybody?

CAL. Mr. Horace he got an attack. He's bad. Miss Regina says you stop that noise.

LEO. Uncle Horace —— What—(*Crosses* U. C.) what happened? (CAL *starts downstairs.* CAL *shakes his head, begins to move swiftly* L. *off.* LEO *looks around wildly.*) But when —— You seen Mr. Oscar or Mr. Ben? (CAL *shakes his head. Moves on.* LEO *grabs him by the arm.*) Answer me, will you?

CAL. No, ain't seen 'em. I ain't got time to answer you. (CAL *breaks* LEO'S *hold, crosses* L.) I got to get things. (CAL *exits.*)

LEO. But what's the matter with him? When did this happen ——? (*Crossing to door* L., *calling after* CAL.) You'd think Papa'd be some place where you could find him. I been chasing him all afternoon. (OSCAR *and* BEN *come swiftly into the room, talking excitedly.*)

OSCAR. I hope it's not a bad attack.

BEN. It's the first one he's had since he come home. (LEO *crosses to* OSCAR, *excitedly.*)

LEO. Papa, I've been looking all over town for you and Uncle Ben ——

67

BEN. Where is he?

OSCAR. Addie said it was sudden.

BEN. (*To* LEO.) Where is he? When did it happen?

LEO. Upstairs. Will you listen to me, please? I been looking for you for ——

OSCAR. (*To* BEN.) You think we should go up? (BEN, *looking up steps, shakes his head.*)

BEN. I don't know. I don't know.

OSCAR. (*Shakes his head.*) But he was all right ——

LEO. (*Almost yelling—turns, crosses* D. *to front chair* L. C.) Will you listen to me?

OSCAR. (*Sharply—crossing* D. *to* LEO.) What is the matter with you?

LEO. (*Coming to him.*) I been trying to tell you. I been trying to find you for an hour ——

OSCAR. Tell me what?

LEO. Uncle Horace knows about the bonds. He knows about them. He's had the box since Wednesday ——

BEN. (*Sharply.*) Stop shouting! (*Crosses* D. C. *to him.*) What the hell are you talking about?

LEO. (*Furiously. Crossing to* BEN.) I'm telling you he knows about the bonds. Ain't that clear enough ——?

OSCAR. (*Grabbing* LEO'S *arm.*) You God damn fool! Stop screaming!

BEN. Now what happened? Talk quietly.

LEO. (*Closes his eyes, angrily, attempted patience.*) You heard me. Uncle Horace knows about the bonds. He's known since Wednesday.

BEN. (*After a second.* OSCAR *draws close to them.*) How do you know that?

LEO. Because Cal comes down to Mander and says the box came O. K. and ——

OSCAR. (*Trembling, crosses to* BEN, *pushing* LEO *away* L.) That might not mean a thing ——

LEO. (*Angrily steps* D. *to* L. *of* OSCAR.) No? It might not, huh? (*Takes* OSCAR'S *arm.* OSCAR *turns to him.*) Then he says Mander should come here tonight and bring Sol Fowler with him. (BEN *crosses* R. *to* R. *of table.*) I guess that don't mean a thing either. (LEO *turns—crosses* D. L.)

68

OSCAR. (*Panicky, to* BEN.) Ben—what —— Do you think he's seen the ——

BEN. (*Motions to box.*) There's the box. (*Both* OSCAR *and* LEO *turn sharply.* LEO *makes a leap to the box, crossing* R. *back of* OSCAR, *picks up box.*) You ass. Put it down. What are you going to do with it, eat it?

LEO. I'm going to —— (*Starts.*)

BEN. (*Furiously.*) Put it down. Don't touch it again. Now sit down and shut up for a minute. (LEO *puts box down on table.*)

OSCAR. (*Crossing to* LEO.) Since Wednesday. (*To* LEO.) You said he had it since Wednesday. Why didn't he say something —— (*To* BEN.) I don't understand ——

LEO. (*Taking a step* R.) I can put it back. I can put it back before anybody knows.

BEN. (*Who is standing at the table* R., *softly.*) He's had it since Wednesday. Yet he hasn't said a word to us.

OSCAR. *Why? Why?*

LEO. What's the difference why? He was getting ready to say plenty. He was going to say it to Fowler tonight ——

OSCAR. (*Angrily.*) Be still. (*Turns to* BEN, *looks at him, waits.*)

BEN. (*After a moment.*) I don't believe that.

LEO. (*Wildly, leaning toward* BEN *over table.*) *You* don't believe it? What do I care what *you* believe? I do the dirty work and then ——

BEN. (*Turning his head sharply to* LEO.) I'm remembering that. I'm remembering that, Leo.

OSCAR. (*A step* D.) What do you mean?

LEO. You ——

BEN. (*To* OSCAR.) If you don't shut that little fool up, I'll show you what I mean. (OSCAR *makes a gesture at* LEO. LEO *crosses* U. C.) For some reason he knows, but he don't say a word.

OSCAR. (*Crossing to* BEN.) Maybe he didn't know that *we* ——

BEN. (*Quickly.*) That *Leo* ——? (*Crosses* C.) He's no fool. (*Crossing up to* LEO.) Does Mander know the bonds are missing?

LEO. How could I tell? I was half crazy. I don't think so. Because Mander seemed kind of puzzled and ——

OSCAR. But we got to find out —— (*He breaks off as* CAL *comes into the room carrying a kettle of hot water and clean cloths, leaving door open. They turn to* CAL. LEO, *startled, crosses* U. L. *to back of settee.*)

BEN. (Crosses to above chair L.) How is he, Cal?

CAL. I don't know, Mr. Ben. He was bad. (Going toward stairs.)

OSCAR. (Crosses L. to chair L.) But when did it happen?

CAL. (Shrugs.) He wasn't feeling so bad early. (ADDIE comes in quickly from hall.) Then there he is next thing on the landing, fallen over, his eyes tight —— (He hurries toward stairs.)

ADDIE. (To CAL.) Dr. Sloan's over at the Ballongs'. Hitch the buggy and go get him. (She takes kettle and cloths from him, pushes him, runs up stairs.) Go on. (She disappears. CAL exits L., picking up his umbrella as he goes. OSCAR crosses D. R.)

BEN. (Takes off coat and hat, places them on chair U. C.) Never seen Sloan anywhere when you need him.

OSCAR. (Softly.) Sounds bad.

LEO. (Taking a step to BEN.) He would have told her about it. Aunt Regina. He would have told his own wife ——

BEN. (Turning to LEO.) Yes, he might have told her. (Crossing to front wheel chair.) But they weren't on such pretty terms and maybe he didn't. Maybe he didn't. (Goes quickly to LEO.) Now, listen to me. If she doesn't know, it may work out all right. (Holding LEO's lapel.) If she does know, you're to say he lent you the bonds.

LEO. Lent them to me! Who's going to believe that?

BEN. Nobody.

OSCAR. (To LEO, crossing to BEN.) Don't you understand? It can't do no harm to say it —— (BEN releases grip on LEO's lapel.)

LEO. Why should I say he lent them to me? Why not to you? (Carefully.) Why not to Uncle Ben?

BEN. (Smiles.) Just because he didn't lend them to me. Remember that.

LEO. But all he has to do is say he didn't lend them to me ——

BEN. (Furiously.) But for some reason, he doesn't seem to be talking, does he? (There are footsteps above. They all stand looking at stairs. REGINA begins to come slowly down. BEN crosses U. R., to REGINA.) What happened?

REGINA. He's had a bad attack. (Crosses D. C.)

OSCAR. Too bad. I'm so sorry we weren't here when—when Horace needed us.

BEN. (Crosses D. C.) When you needed us.

REGINA. (At chair L. C. Looks at him.) Yes.

BEN. How is he? Can we—can we go up?

70

REGINA. (*Shakes her head.*) He's not conscious.

OSCAR. (*Pacing around.*) It's that—it's that bad? (*Turns, crosses* D. R.) Wouldn't you think Sloan could be found quickly, just once, just once?

REGINA. I don't think there is much for him to do.

BEN. (*Crossing to* REGINA.) Oh, don't talk like that. He's come through attacks before. He will now. (REGINA *sits down, chair* L. C. *After a second she speaks softly.* LEO *crosses* R. *to above table* R.)

REGINA. Well. We haven't seen each other since the day of our fight.

BEN. (*Tenderly.*) That was nothing. Why, you and Oscar and I used to fight when we were kids.

OSCAR. (*Hurriedly taking a step* L.) Don't you think we should go up? Is there anything we can do for Horace ——

BEN. You don't feel well. Ah ——

REGINA. (*Without looking at them.*) No, I don't. (*Slight pause.*) Horace told me about the bonds this afternoon. (*There is an immediate shocked silence.*)

LEO. (*Taking several short steps to* L. *of table* R.) The bonds. What do you mean? What bonds? What ——?

OSCAR. (*Looks at him furiously. Then to* REGINA.) The Union Pacific bonds? Horace's Union Pacific bonds?

REGINA. Yes.

OSCAR. (*Step to her, very nervously.*) Well. Well, what—what about them? What—what could he say?

REGINA. He said that Leo had stolen the bonds and given them to you.

OSCAR. (*Aghast, very loudly.*) That's ridiculous, Regina, absolutely ——

LEO. I don't know what you're talking about. What would I— why ——

REGINA. (*Wearily to* BEN.) Isn't it enough that he stole them from me? Do I have to listen to this in the bargain?

OSCAR. You are talking ——

LEO. I didn't steal anything. I don't know why ——

REGINA. (*To* BEN.) Would you ask them to stop that, please? (*Silence for a minute.* BEN *glowers at* OSCAR *and* LEO, LEO *looks at* OSCAR.)

71

BEN. Aren't we starting at the wrong end, Regina? What did Horace tell you?

REGINA. (*Smiles at him.*) He told me that Leo had stolen the bonds.

LEO. (*To* BEN.) I didn't steal ——

REGINA. Please. Let me finish. (LEO *crosses* R. *slowly.*) Then he told me that he was going to pretend that he had lent them to you (LEO *turns sharply to* REGINA, *then looks at* OSCAR, *then looks back at* REGINA.) as a present from me to my brothers. He said there was nothing I could do about it. He said the rest of his money would go to Alexandra. That is all. (*Silence.* OSCAR *coughs,* LEO *smiles slyly.*)

LEO. (*Taking a step to her.*) I told you he had lent them—I could have told you ——

REGINA. (*Ignores him, smiles sadly at* BEN.) So I'm very badly off, you see. (*Carefully.*) But Horace said there was nothing I could do about it as long as he was alive to say he had lent you the bonds.

BEN. You shouldn't feel that way. It can all be explained, all be adjusted. It isn't as bad ——

REGINA. So you, at least, are willing to admit that the bonds were stolen?

BEN. (*Laughs.* OSCAR *laughs nervously.*) I admit no such thing. It's possible that Horace made up that part of the story to tease you —— (*Looks at her.*) Or perhaps to punish you. Punish you.

REGINA. (*Sadly.*) It's not a pleasant story. I feel bad, Ben, naturally. I hadn't thought ——

BEN. Now you shall have the bonds safely back. That was the understanding, wasn't it, Oscar?

OSCAR. (*Crossing to* C.) Yes.

REGINA. I'm glad to know that. (*Smiles.*) Ah, I had greater hopes ——

BEN. Don't talk that way. That's foolish. (*Looks at his watch.*) I think we ought to drive out for Sloan ourselves. (*Looks at* OSCAR.) If we can't find him we'll go over to Senateville for Doctor Morris. (*Looks at her.* OSCAR *crosses* U. *to chair* R. C. *for hat,* LEO *crosses* U. *back of sofa to hall, picking up hat.*) And don't think I'm dismissing this other business. I'm not. We'll have it all out on a more appropriate day. (BEN *crosses* U. *to chair* U C. *for coat and hat.*)

REGINA. (*Waits until they are near door. Looks up, quietly.*) I don't think you had better go yet. I think you had better stay and sit down. (OSCAR *crosses to hall.*)

BEN. (*Picking up coat and hat.*) We'll be back with Sloan.

REGINA. Cal has gone for him. I don't want you to go. (OSCAR *turns, looks at them.*)

BEN. (*Crossing* U. C.) Now don't worry and ——

REGINA. You will come back in this room and sit down. I have something more to say. (LEO *steps back into view.*)

BEN. (*Turns, comes toward her to* C.) Since when do I take orders from you?

REGINA. (*Smiles.*) You don't—yet. (OSCAR *takes a step in. Sharply.*) Come back, Oscar. You too, Leo.

OSCAR. (*Takes another step in. Sure of himself, laughs.*) My dear Regina ——

BEN. (*Crosses to her. Softly, pats her hand.*) Horace has already clipped your wings and very wittily. Do I have to clip them, too? (*Smiles at her.*) You'd get farther with a smile, Regina. I'm a soft man for a woman's smile.

REGINA. I'm smiling, Ben, I'm smiling because you are quite safe while Horace lives. But I don't think Horace will live. (LEO *looks at* OSCAR. *To* BEN.) And if he doesn't live I shall want seventy-five per cent in exchange for the bonds.

BEN. (*Steps back. Whistles, laughs.*) Greedy! What a greedy girl you are! You want so much of everything.

REGINA. Yes. And if I don't get what I want I am going to put all three of you in jail.

OSCAR. (*Crosses* L. *to* R. *of* REGINA, *furiously.*) You're mighty crazy. Having just admitted —— (LEO *steps* D.)

BEN. And on what evidence would you put Oscar and Leo in jail?

REGINA. (*Laughs, gaily.*) Oscar, listen to him. He's getting ready to swear that it was you and Leo! What do you say to that? (*As* OSCAR *turns furiously toward* BEN.) Oh, don't be angry, Oscar. I'm going to see that he goes in with you. (OSCAR *turns, steps* U. C.)

BEN. Try anything you like, Regina. (*Steps to* REGINA. OSCAR *crosses* U. R. *Sharply.*) And now we can stop all this and say good-bye to you. (ALEXANDRA *comes into view on landing, moving slowly down steps.*) It's his money and he's obviously willing to let us borrow it. (*More pleasantly.* LEO *slowly crosses* U. *to hall.*) Learn to make threats when you can carry them through: for how

73

many years have I told you a good-looking woman gets more by being soft and appealing? Mama used to tell you that. (*Looks at his watch.*) Where the hell is Sloan? (*To* OSCAR.) Take the buggy and —— (*As* BEN *turns to* OSCAR, *he sees* ALEXANDRA *and stops.* OSCAR *turns to her.* ALEXANDRA *has come slowly down the steps. She walks stiffly. She comes down as if she did not see any of them. She goes slowly to lower window, her head bent. They all turn to look at her.*)

OSCAR. (*After a second, moving toward her above sofa.*) What? Alexandra —— (*She does not answer. After a second* ADDIE *comes slowly downstairs, moving as if she were very tired. At foot of steps, she looks at* ALEXANDRA, *then turns and slowly crosses to door* L. *and exits.* REGINA *rises. She sees* ADDIE. BEN *looks nervously at* ALEXANDRA, *at* REGINA. OSCAR, *as* ADDIE *passes him, irritably, to* ALEXANDRA.) Well, what is—(*Turns into room—sees* ADDIE *at foot of steps.*) what's ——? (BEN *puts up a hand, shakes head. His movements become nervous and fidgety, as if he were anxious to get out.* OSCAR *clears his throat, looks at* REGINA, *tries to fill the silence.* LEO *steps* D.) My God, I didn't know—who could have known—I didn't know he was that sick. Well, well—I —— (REGINA *stands quietly, her back to them.*)

BEN. (*Softly, sincerely.*) Seems like yesterday when he first came here. (*Places coat and hat on chair above wheel chair.*)

OSCAR. (*Sincerely, nervously.*) Yes, that's true. (*Turns to* BEN.) The whole town loved him and respected him.

ALEXANDRA. (*Turns and crosses to below sofa* R.) Did you love him, Uncle Oscar?

OSCAR. (*Turns to* ALEXANDRA.) Certainly, I —— What a strange thing to ask. I ——

ALEXANDRA. (*Turns to look at* BEN.) Did you love him, Uncle Ben?

BEN. (*Simply.*) He had ——

ALEXANDRA. (*Suddenly starts to laugh very loudly.*) And you, Mama, did you love him, too?

REGINA. I know what you feel, Alexandra, but please try to control yourself.

ALEXANDRA. (*Still laughing.*) I'm trying, Mama. I'm trying very hard.

BEN. Grief makes some people laugh and some people cry. It's better to cry, Alexandra.

ALEXANDRA. (*The laugh has stopped. Tensely. Moves toward* REGINA, *crossing to front sofa.*) What was Papa doing on the staircase?

REGINA. (*Crossing R. to* ALEXANDRA. BEN *turns to look at* ALEXANDRA *with interest.*) Please go and lie down, my dear. We all need time to get over shocks like this. (ALEXANDRA *does not move.* REGINA'S *voice becomes softer, more insistent.*) Please go, Alexandra.

ALEXANDRA. No, Mama. I'll wait. I've got to talk to you.

REGINA. Later. Go and rest now.

ALEXANDRA. (*Quietly.*) I'll wait, Mama. I've plenty of time. (*Sits down on sofa.*) All my life.

REGINA. (*Hesitates, stares, makes a half shrug, turns back to* BEN, *crossing L. to* C.) As I was saying. Tomorrow morning I am going up to Judge Simmes. I shall tell him about Leo.

BEN. (*Motioning toward* ALEXANDRA, *steps D. to chair* L.C.) Not in front of the child, Regina. I ——

REGINA. (*Turns to him. Sharply.*) I didn't ask her to stay. (*Turns away, crossing L.*) Tomorrow morning I go to Judge Simmes ——

OSCAR. And what proof? What proof of all this ——

REGINA. (*Turns, crosses to* C. *between* BEN *and* OSCAR. *To* OSCAR *sharply.*) None. I won't need any. The bonds are missing and they are with Marshall. That will be enough. If it isn't, I'll add what's necessary.

BEN. I'm sure of that.

REGINA. (*Turns to* BEN.) You can be quite sure.

OSCAR. We'll deny ——

REGINA. Deny your heads off. You couldn't find a jury that wouldn't weep for a woman whose brothers steal from her. *And* you couldn't find twelve men in this State you haven't cheated and hate you for it.

OSCAR. What kind of talk is this? You couldn't do anything like that! We're your own brothers. How can you talk that way when upstairs not five minutes ago —— (*Points upstairs.*)

REGINA. (*Slowly.*) There are people who can never go back, who must finish what they start. I am one of those people, Oscar. (*After a slight pause, turns back to* BEN, *almost teasingly.*) Where was I? (*Smiles at* BEN.) Well, they'll convict you. But I won't care much if they don't. (*Leans forward, pleasantly.*) Because by that time you'll be ruined. (*Crosses D. L.*) I shall also tell my story to

Mr. Marshall, who likes me, I think, and who will not want to be involved in your scandal. A respectable firm like Marshall & Company! The deal would be off in an hour. (*Turns to them angrily.*) And you know it. Now I don't want to hear any more from any of you. *You'll do no more bargaining in this house.* I'll take my seventy-five per cent and we'll forget the story forever. That's one way of doing it, and the way I prefer. (*Crosses to settee L.*) You know me well enough to know that I don't mind taking the other way. (*Sits down on settee.*)

BEN. (*After a second, slowly, at chair L. C.*) None of us have ever known you well enough, Regina.

REGINA. You're getting old, Ben. Your tricks aren't as smart as they used to be. (*There is no answer. She waits, then smiles.*) All right. I take it that's settled and I get what I asked for.

OSCAR. (*Furiously to* BEN.) Are you going to let her do this ———?

BEN. (*Turns to look at him, slowly.*) You have a suggestion?

REGINA. (*Puts her arms above her head, stretches, laughs.*) No, he hasn't. All right. Now, Leo, I have forgotten that you ever saw the bonds. (*Archly, to* BEN *and* OSCAR.) And as long as you boys both behave yourselves, I've forgotten that we ever talked about them. You can draw up the necessary papers tomorrow. (BEN *laughs.* LEO *stares at him, starts for door. Exits.* OSCAR *moves toward door, angrily.* REGINA *looks at* BEN, *nods, laughs with him. For a second,* OSCAR *stands in door, looking back at them. Then he exits.*) You're a good loser, Ben. I like that.

BEN. (*He picks up his coat, then turns to her.*) Well, I say to myself, what's the good? You and I aren't like Oscar. We're not sour people. I think that comes from a good digestion. (*Putting on coat.*) Then, too, one loses today and wins tomorrow. I say to myself, years of planning and I get what I want. Then I don't get it. But I'm not discouraged. The century's turning, the world is open. Open for people like you and me. Ready for us, waiting for us. After all, this is just the beginning. (*Crosses L. to above chair L. C.*) There are hundreds of Hubbards sitting in rooms like this throughout the country. All their names aren't Hubbard, but they are all Hubbards and they will own this country some day. We'll get along.

REGINA. (*Smiles.*) I think so.

BEN. (*Crosses to chair, picks up hat.*) Then, too, I say to myself, things may change. (*Looks at* ALEXANDRA.) I agree with Alex·

andra. (*Looks up at landing.*) What is a man in a wheel chair doing on a staircase? I ask myself that.

REGINA. (*Looks up at him.*) And what do you answer?

BEN. I have no answer. (*Crosses L. to back of settee.*) But maybe some day I will. Maybe never, but maybe some day. (*Smiles. Patting her arm.*) When I do, I'll let you know. (*Crosses to C., toward hall.*)

REGINA. (*As he turns for door.*) When you do, write me. I will be in Chicago. (*Gaily.*) Ah, Ben, if Papa had only left me his money.

BEN. I'll see you tomorrow. (*Crosses R. to above wheel chair.*)

REGINA. Oh, yes. Certainly. You'll be sort of working for me now.

BEN. (*Turns, crosses to above sofa R., looks at ALEXANDRA, smiles at her.*) Alexandra, you're turning out to be a right interesting girl. (*Looks at REGINA.*) Well, good night, all. (*He exits.*)

REGINA. (*Sits quietly for a second, stretches, turns to look at ALEXANDRA.*) What do you want to talk to me about, Alexandra?

ALEXANDRA. (*Slowly.*) I've changed my mind. I don't want to talk. There's nothing to talk about now.

REGINA. You're acting very strange. Not like yourself. You've had a bad shock today. I know that. And you loved Papa, but you must have expected this to come some day. You knew how sick he was.

ALEXANDRA. I knew. We all knew.

REGINA. It will be good for you to get away from here. Good for me, too. Time heals most wounds, Alexandra. You're young, you shall have all the things I wanted. I'll make the world for you the way I wanted it to be for me. (*Uncomfortably.*) Don't sit there staring. You've been around Birdie so much you're getting just like her.

ALEXANDRA. (*Nods.*) Funny. That's what Aunt Birdie said today.

REGINA. (*Nods.*) Be good for you to get away from all this. (ADDIE *enters.*)

ADDIE. Cal is back, Miss Regina. He says Dr. Sloan will be coming in a few minutes.

REGINA. We'll go in a few weeks. A few weeks! That means two or three Saturdays, two or three Sundays. (*Sighs.*) Well, I'm very tired. I shall go to bed. I don't want any supper. Put the lights out and lock up. (ADDIE *moves to the piano lamp, turns it out.*) You go to your room, Alexandra. Addie will bring you something hot. You look very tired. (*Rises, crosses U. C. To ADDIE.*) Call me when

Dr. Sloan gets here. I don't want to see anybody else. I don't want any condolence calls tonight. The whole town will be over.

ALEXANDRA. Mama, I'm not coming with you. I'm not going to Chicago.

REGINA. (*Turns to her.*) You're very upset, Alexandra.

ALEXANDRA. (*Quietly.*) I mean what I say. With all my heart.

REGINA. (*Quietly.*) We'll talk about it tomorrow. The morning will make a difference.

ALEXANDRA. It won't make any difference. And there isn't anything to talk about. I am going away from you. Because I want to. Because I know Papa would want me to.

REGINA. (*Puzzled, careful, polite.*) You *know* your Papa wanted you to go away from me?

ALEXANDRA. Yes.

REGINA. (*Softly.*) And if I say no?

ALEXANDRA. (*Looks at her, firmly.*) Say it, Mama, say it. And see what happens.

REGINA. (*Softly, after a pause.*) And if I make you stay?

ALEXANDRA. That would be foolish. It wouldn't work in the end.

REGINA. You're very serious about it, aren't you? (*Crosses to steps —up two steps.*) Well, you'll change your mind in a few days.

ALEXANDRA. You only change your mind when you want to. And I won't want to.

REGINA. (*Going up steps.*) Alexandra, I've come to the end of my rope. (*On fifth step.*) Somewhere there has to be what I want, too. Life goes too fast. Do what you want; think what you want; go where you want. I'd like to keep you with me, but I won't make you stay. Too many people used to make me do too many things. No. (*Going up to landing.*) I won't make you stay.

ALEXANDRA. You couldn't, Mama, because I want to leave here. As I've never wanted anything in my life before. Because I understand what Papa was trying to tell me. (*Pause.*) All in one day: Addie said there were people who ate the earth and other people who stood around and watched them do it. And just now Uncle Ben said the same thing. Really, he said the same thing. (*Tensely.*) Well, tell him for me, Mama, I'm not going to stand around and watch you do it. Tell him I'll be fighting as hard as he'll be fighting (*Rises, step* u. *to table.*) some place where people don't just stand around and watch.

REGINA. Well, you have spirit, after all. I used to think you were

all sugar water. We don't have to be bad friends. I don't want us to be bad friends, Alexandra. (*Starts off, stops, turns to* ALEXANDRA.) Would you like to come and talk to me, Alexandra? Would you—would you like to sleep in my room tonight?
ALEXANDRA. (*Takes a step toward her.*) Are you afraid, Mama? (REGINA *does not answer, but moves slowly out of sight.* ADDIE *then comes to* ALEXANDRA, *squeezes her arm with affection and pride, then starts for other lamp, as*)

THE CURTAIN FALLS

PROPERTIES

Wine glasses
Bottle of port
Tray
Brooms
Mops
Rags
Dustpan
Large silver tray with coffee urn, small cups, coffee articles, and newspaper
Newspaper (another)
Several packages
Small package of medicine (bottle inside), spoon for medicine
Napkin
Biscuit
Glass of water
Small safe deposit box
Sewing basket with sewing articles in it
Small hand towel (kitchen)
Large tray (with glasses)
Canape with elderberry wine
Plate with cookies
Torn umbrella
Kettle of hot water
Cloths

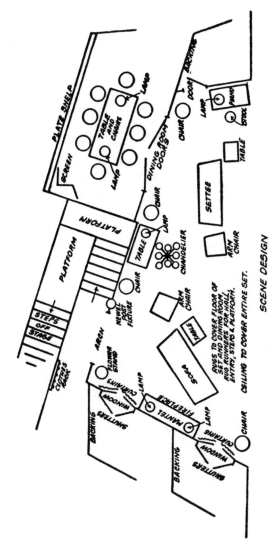

SCENE DESIGN

"THE LITTLE FOXES"

NEW PLAYS

★ **HONOUR by Joanna Murray-Smith.** In a series of intense confrontations, a wife, husband, lover and daughter negotiate the forces of passion, history, responsibility and honour. "HONOUR makes for surprisingly interesting viewing. Tight, crackling dialogue (usually played out in punchy verbal duels) captures characters unable to deal with emotions ... Murray-Smith effectively places her characters in situations that strip away pretense." –*Variety* "... the play's virtues are strong: a distinctive theatrical voice, passionate concerns ... HONOUR might just capture a few honors of its own." –*Time Out Magazine* [1M, 3W] ISBN: 0-8222-1683-3

★ **MR. PETERS' CONNECTIONS by Arthur Miller.** Mr. Miller describes the protagonist as existing in a dream-like state when the mind is "freed to roam from real memories to conjectures, from trivialities to tragic insights, from terror of death to glorying in one's being alive." With this memory play, the Tony Award and Pulitzer Prize-winner reaffirms his stature as the world's foremost dramatist. "... a cross between Joycean stream-of-consciousness and Strindberg's dream plays, sweetened with a dose of William Saroyan's philosophical whimsy ... CONNECTIONS is most intriguing ..." –*The NY Times* [5M, 3W] ISBN: 0-8222-1687-6

★ **THE WAITING ROOM by Lisa Loomer.** Three women from different centuries meet in a doctor's waiting room in this dark comedy about the timeless quest for beauty – and its cost. "... THE WAITING ROOM ... is a bold, risky melange of conflicting elements that is ... terrifically moving ... There's no resisting the fierce emotional pull of the play." –*The NY Times* "... one of the high points of this year's Off-Broadway season ... THE WAITING ROOM is well worth a visit." –*Back Stage* [7M, 4W, flexible casting] ISBN: 0-8222-1594-2

★ **THE OLD SETTLER by John Henry Redwood.** A sweet-natured comedy about two church-going sisters in 1943 Harlem and the handsome young man who rents a room in their apartment. "For all of its decent sentiments, THE OLD SETTLER avoids sentimentality. It has the authenticity and lack of pretense of an Early American sampler." –*The NY Times* "We've had some fine plays Off-Broadway this season, and this is one of the best." –*The NY Post* [1M, 3W] ISBN: 0-8-222-1642-6

★ **LAST TRAIN TO NIBROC by Arlene Hutton.** In 1940 two young strangers share a seat on a train bound east only to find their paths will cross again. "All aboard. LAST TRAIN TO NIBROC is a sweetly told little chamber romance." –*Show Business* "... [a] gently charming little play, reminiscent of Thornton Wilder in its look at rustic Americans who are to be treasured for their simplicity and directness ..." –*Associated Press* "The old formula of boy wins girls, boy loses girl, boy wins girl still works ... [a] well-made play that perfectly captures a slice of small-town-life-gone-by." –*Back Stage* [1M, 1W] ISBN: 0-8222-1753-8

★ **OVER THE RIVER AND THROUGH THE WOODS by Joe DiPietro.** Nick sees both sets of his grandparents every Sunday for dinner. This is routine until he has to tell them that he's been offered a dream job in Seattle. The news doesn't sit so well. "A hilarious family comedy that is even funnier than his long running musical revue *I Love You, You're Perfect, Now Change.*" –*Back Stage* "Loaded with laughs every step of the way." –*Star-Ledger* [3M, 3W] ISBN: 0-8222-1712-0

★ **SIDE MAN by Warren Leight.** 1999 Tony Award winner. This is the story of a broken family and the decline of jazz as popular entertainment. "... a tender, deeply personal memory play about the turmoil in the family of a jazz musician as his career crumbles at the dawn of the age of rock-and-roll ..." –*The NY Times* "[SIDE MAN] is an elegy for two things – a lost world and a lost love. When the two notes sound together in harmony, it is moving and graceful ..." –*The NY Daily News* "An atmospheric memory play ... with crisp dialogue and clearly drawn characters ... reflects the passing of an era with persuasive insight ... The joy and despair of the musicians is skillfully illustrated." –*Variety* [5M, 3W] ISBN: 0-8222-1721-X

DRAMATISTS PLAY SERVICE, INC.
440 Park Avenue South, New York, NY 10016 212-683-8960 Fax 212-213-1539
postmaster@dramatists.com www.dramatists.com

NEW PLAYS

★ **CLOSER by Patrick Marber.** Winner of the 1998 Olivier Award for Best Play and the 1999 New York Drama Critics Circle Award for Best Foreign Play. Four lives intertwine over the course of four and a half years in this densely plotted, stinging look at modern love and betrayal. "CLOSER is a sad, savvy, often funny play that casts a steely, unblinking gaze at the world of relationships and lets you come to your own conclusions ... CLOSER does not merely hold your attention; it burrows into you." –*New York Magazine* "A powerful, darkly funny play about the cosmic collision between the sun of love and the comet of desire." –*Newsweek Magazine* [2M, 2W] ISBN: 0-8222-1722-8

★ **THE MOST FABULOUS STORY EVER TOLD by Paul Rudnick.** A stage manager, headset and prompt book at hand, brings the house lights to half, then dark, and cues the creation of the world. Throughout the play, she's in control of everything. In other words, she's either God, or she thinks she is. "Line by line, Mr. Rudnick may be the funniest writer for the stage in the United States today ... One-liners, epigrams, withering put-downs and flashing repartee: These are the candles that Mr. Rudnick lights instead of cursing the darkness ... a testament to the virtues of laughing ... and in laughter, there is something like the memory of Eden." –*The NY Times* "Funny it is ... consistently, rapaciously, deliriously ... easily the funniest play in town." –*Variety* [4M, 5W] ISBN: 0-8222-1720-1

★ **A DOLL'S HOUSE by Henrik Ibsen, adapted by Frank McGuinness.** Winner of the 1997 Tony Award for Best Revival. "New, raw, gut-twisting and gripping. Easily the hottest drama this season." –*USA Today* "Bold, brilliant and alive." –*The Wall Street Journal* "A thunderclap of an evening that takes your breath away." –*Time Magazine* [4M, 4W, 2 boys] ISBN: 0-8222-1636-1

★ **THE HERBAL BED by Peter Whelan.** The play is based on actual events which occurred in Stratford-upon-Avon in the summer of 1613, when William Shakespeare's elder daughter was publicly accused of having a sexual liaison with a married neighbor and family friend. "In his probing new play, THE HERBAL BED ... Peter Whelan muses about a sidelong event in the life of Shakespeare's family and creates a finely textured tapestry of love and lies in the early 17th-century Stratford." –*The NY Times* "It is a first rate drama with interesting moral issues of truth and expediency." –*The NY Post* [5M, 3W] ISBN: 0-8222-1675-2

★ **SNAKEBIT by David Marshall Grant.** A study of modern friendship when put to the test. "... a rather smart and absorbing evening of water-cooler theater, the intimate sort of Off-Broadway experience that has you picking apart the recognizable characters long after the curtain calls." –*The NY Times* "Off-Broadway keeps on presenting us with compelling reasons for going to the theater. The latest is SNAKEBIT, David Marshall Grant's smart new comic drama about being thirtysomething and losing one's way in life." –*The NY Daily News* [3M, 1W] ISBN: 0-8222-1724-4

★ **A QUESTION OF MERCY by David Rabe.** The Obie Award-winning playwright probes the sensitive and controversial issue of doctor-assisted suicide in the age of AIDS in this poignant drama. "There are many devastating ironies in Mr. Rabe's beautifully considered, piercingly clear-eyed work ..." –*The NY Times* "With unsettling candor and disturbing insight, the play arouses pity and understanding of a troubling subject ... Rabe's provocative tale is an affirmation of dignity that rings clear and true." –*Variety* [6M, 1W] ISBN: 0-8222-1643-4

★ **DIMLY PERCEIVED THREATS TO THE SYSTEM by Jon Klein.** Reality and fantasy overlap with hilarious results as this unforgettable family attempts to survive the nineties. "Here's a play whose point about fractured families goes to the heart, mind – and ears." –*The Washington Post* "... an end-of-the-millennium comedy about a family on the verge of a nervous breakdown ... Trenchant and hilarious ..." –*The Baltimore Sun* [2M, 4W] ISBN: 0-8222-1677-9

DRAMATISTS PLAY SERVICE, INC.
440 Park Avenue South, New York, NY 10016 212-683-8960 Fax 212-213-1539
postmaster@dramatists.com www.dramatists.com

NEW PLAYS

★ **AS BEES IN HONEY DROWN by Douglas Carter Beane.** Winner of the John Gassner Playwriting Award. A hot young novelist finds the subject of his new screenplay in a New York socialite who leads him into the world of *Auntie Mame* and *Breakfast at Tiffany's*, before she takes him for a ride. "A delicious soufflé of a satire … [an] extremely entertaining fable for an age that always chooses image over substance." *–The NY Times* "… A witty assessment of one of the most active and relentless industries in a consumer society … the creation of 'hot' young things, which the media have learned to mass produce with efficiency and zeal." *–The NY Daily News* [3M, 3W, flexible casting] ISBN: 0-8222-1651-5

★ **STUPID KIDS by John C. Russell.** In rapid, highly stylized scenes, the story follows four high-school students as they make their way from first through eighth period and beyond, struggling with the fears, frustrations, and longings peculiar to youth. "In STUPID KIDS … playwright John C. Russell gets the opera of adolescence to a T … The stylized teenspeak of STUPID KIDS … suggests that Mr. Russell may have hidden a tape recorder under a desk in study hall somewhere and then scoured the tapes for good quotations … it is the kids' insular, ceaselessly churning world, a pre-adult world of Doritos and libidos, that the playwright seeks to lay bare." *–The NY Times* "STUPID KIDS [is] a sharp-edged … whoosh of teen angst and conformity anguish. It is also very funny." *–NY Newsday* [2M, 2W] ISBN: 0-8222-1698-1

★ **COLLECTED STORIES by Donald Margulies.** From Obie Award-winner Donald Margulies comes a provocative analysis of a student-teacher relationship that turns sour when the protégé becomes a rival. "With his fine ear for detail, Margulies creates an authentic, insular world, and he gives equal weight to the opposing viewpoints of two formidable characters." *–The LA Times* "This is probably Margulies' best play to date …" *–The NY Post* "… always fluid and lively, the play is thick with ideas, like a stock-pot of good stew." *–The Village Voice* [2W] ISBN: 0-8222-1640-X

★ **FREEDOMLAND by Amy Freed.** An overdue showdown between a son and his father sets off fireworks that illuminate the neurosis, rage and anxiety of one family – and of America at the turn of the millennium. "FREEDOMLAND's more obvious links are to *Buried Child* and *Bosoms and Neglect*. Freed, like Guare, is an inspired wordsmith with a gift for surreal touches in situations grounded in familiar and real territory." *–Curtain Up* [3M, 4W] ISBN: 0-8222-1719-8

★ **STOP KISS by Diana Son.** A poignant and funny play about the ways, both sudden and slow, that lives can change irrevocably. "There's so much that is vital and exciting about STOP KISS … you want to embrace this young author and cheer her onto other works … the writing on display here is funny and credible … you also will be charmed by its heartfelt characters and up-to-the-minute humor." *–The NY Daily News* "… irresistibly exciting … a sweet, sad, and enchantingly sincere play." *–The NY Times* [3M, 3W] ISBN: 0-8222-1731-7

★ **THREE DAYS OF RAIN by Richard Greenberg.** The sins of fathers and mothers make for a bittersweet elegy in this poignant and revealing drama. "… a work so perfectly judged it heralds the arrival of a major playwright … Greenberg is extraordinary." *–The NY Daily News* "Greenberg's play is filled with graceful passages that are by turns melancholy, harrowing, and often, quite funny." *–Variety* [2M, 1W] ISBN: 0-8222-1676-0

★ **THE WEIR by Conor McPherson.** In a bar in rural Ireland, the local men swap spooky stories in an attempt to impress a young woman from Dublin who recently moved into a nearby "haunted" house. However, the tables are soon turned when she spins a yarn of her own. "You shed all sense of time at this beautiful and devious new play." *–The NY Times* "Sheer theatrical magic. I have rarely been so convinced that I have just seen a modern classic. Tremendous." *–The London Daily Telegraph* [4M, 1W] ISBN: 0-8222-1706-6

DRAMATISTS PLAY SERVICE, INC.
440 Park Avenue South, New York, NY 10016 212-683-8960 Fax 212-213-1539
postmaster@dramatists.com www.dramatists.com